Walking in Wisdom

An 8-Week Proverbs Bible Study For Women

Bridging The Gaps Ministry Inc.

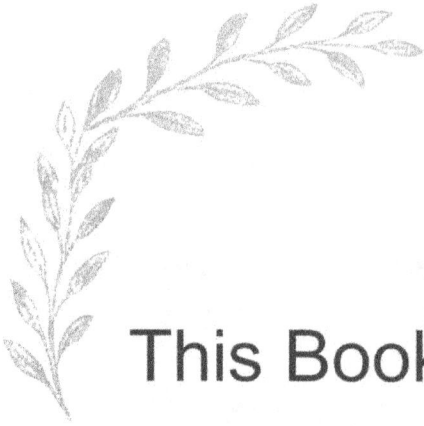

This Book Belongs To:

_____

_____

_____

May God bless your journey through His wisdom

To God be the glory — the Author of wisdom, the Giver of grace, and the One who makes all things beautiful in His time.

Every page of this study exists because of Your guidance, Your patience, and Your unfailing love. Thank You, Lord, for walking with me, teaching me, and sustaining me through every step of this journey.

And to three absolutely **fearfully and wonderfully made** women who have walked beside me with strength, love, and faith —
Lori Lockwood, Faith Cooper, and Kitina Watson —
thank you for believing in me, praying with me, and refusing to let me fall.

Your encouragement, wisdom, and sisterhood have been living reflections of God's grace in motion.

This work is as much yours as it is mine — a testimony of friendship rooted in faith, perseverance, and divine purpose.

"Two are better than one; because they have a good reward for their labour.
For if they fall, the one will lift up his fellow."
— Ecclesiastes 4:9–10 (KJV)

Acknowledgements

First and foremost, I give honor and thanks to God.
For His wisdom, His presence, His unfailing love,
and the privilege of sharing His Word through this study.

To every woman who has prayed for me, encouraged me, or spoken life
into me during this journey — thank you. Your support has helped bring
this project from vision to reality.

To all who will read, share, teach, or lead with this study,
thank you for allowing *Walking in Wisdom* to be a part of your spiritual
growth.

May God bless you richly as you walk deeper in His truth.

With love,
Bridging The Gaps Ministry Inc.

www.BridgingTheGapsInc.com

Thank you for choosing to walk through this study.
Walking in Wisdom was created to help women grow spiritually, renew their minds, and walk confidently in God's guidance.

Proverbs is filled with practical instruction for everyday life — wisdom that strengthens our decisions, shapes our character, and brings clarity in seasons of uncertainty.

Over the next eight weeks, you will:

- Read and reflect on Scripture
- Develop spiritual maturity
- Explore how God's wisdom applies to your daily life
- Strengthen your relationship with Christ
- Practice real, meaningful application

Wherever you are on your spiritual journey — beginning again, rebuilding, recovering, or growing deeper — this study is for you.

My prayer is that during these eight weeks, you will experience God's presence, guidance, and peace in personal and powerful ways.

Let's walk this wisdom journey together.

This study is designed to be simple, flexible, and powerful. Whether you complete it individually or in a group, these steps will help you get the most out of each week.

- **Set Aside Dedicated Time**
  Choose a consistent study time in a quiet place.
- **Pray Before You Begin**
  Invite the Holy Spirit to guide your understanding.
- **Read the Scripture Slowly**
  Use your Bible or the included ASV version.
- **Reflect Deeply**
  Allow the questions to help you pause, process, and apply God's Word.
- **Be Honest and Open**
  God meets you where you are — spiritually, emotionally, and mentally.
- **Apply What You Learn**
  Wisdom becomes transformation when it is lived, not just read.
- **Stay Consistent**
  Your growth will come from steady, intentional time with God.
- **Seek God in Every Step**
  He desires closeness with you.
  Every moment in His Word is an investment in your spiritual life.

For questions, testimonies, or resources, contact:
Contact@bridgingthegapsinc.com

Table of Contents

Let's go!

God is ready to speak -
and wisdom is waiting for you.

Week 1 – The Foundation Of Wisdom

Theme: Beginning with the Fear of the Lord
Weekly Focus: Proverbs 1-3

Let's Pray

Father God, thank You for Your Word that teaches me wisdom. Help me to open my heart this week to understand what it means to respect You and trust You more than my own thoughts. Show me how to walk in Your ways.

In Jesus' name, Amen.

Reading Plan:

☐ **Proverbs 1 – The Purpose of Proverbs & Warning Against Enticement**

1 [1]The proverbs of Solomon the son of David, king of Israel: [2] To know wisdom and instruction; To discern the words of understanding; [3] To receive instruction in wise dealing, In righteousness and justice and equity; [4] To give prudence to the simple, To the young man knowledge and discretion: [5]That the wise man may hear, and increase in learning; And that the man of understanding may attain unto sound counsels: [6] To understand a proverb, and a figure, The words of the wise, and their dark sayings. [7]The fear of Jehovah is the beginning of knowledge; But the foolish despise wisdom and instruction. [8]My son, hear the instruction of thy father, And forsake not the law of thy mother: [9] For they shall be a chaplet of grace unto thy head, And chains about thy neck. [10]My son, if sinners entice thee, Consent thou not. [11] If they say, Come with us, Let us lay wait for blood; Let us lurk privily for the innocent without cause; [12] Let us swallow them up alive as Sheol, And whole, as those that go down into the pit; [13]We shall find all precious substance; We shall fill our houses with spoil; [14] Thou shalt cast thy lot among us; We will all have one purse: [15]My son, walk not thou in the way with them; Refrain thy foot from their path: [16] For their feet run to evil,

And they make haste to shed blood. [17]For in vain is the net spread In the sight of any bird: [18] And these lay wait for their own blood; They lurk privily for their own lives. [19] So are the ways of every one that is greedy of gain; It taketh away the life of the owners thereof. [20]Wisdom crieth aloud in the street; She uttereth her voice in the broad places; [21]She crieth in the chief place of concourse; At the entrance of the gates, In the city, she uttereth her words: [22] How long, ye simple ones, will ye love simplicity? And scoffers delight them in scoffing, And fools hate knowledge? [23] Turn you at my reproof: Behold, I will pour out my spirit upon you; I will make known my words unto you. [24]Because I have called, and ye have refused; I have stretched out my hand, and no man hath regarded; [25]But ye have set at nought all my counsel, And would none of my reproof: [26] I also will laugh in the day of your calamity; I will mock when your fear cometh; [27]When your fear cometh as a storm, And your calamity cometh on as a whirlwind; When distress and anguish come upon you. [28] Then will they call upon me, but I will not answer; They will seek me diligently, but they shall not find me: [29] For that they hated knowledge, And did not choose the fear of Jehovah, [30] They would none of my counsel, They despised all my reproof. [31]Therefore shall they eat of the fruit of their own way, And be filled with their own devices. [32] For the backsliding of the simple shall slay them, And the careless ease of fools shall destroy them. [33]But whoso hearkeneth unto me shall dwell securely, And shall be quiet without fear of evil.

Reading Plan:

☐ **Proverbs 2 – The Value of Wisdom**

2 [1]My son, if thou wilt receive my words, And lay up my commandments with thee; [2] So as to incline thine ear unto wisdom, And apply thy heart to understanding; [3] Yea, if thou cry after discernment, And lift up thy voice for understanding; [4] If thou seek her as silver, And search for her as for hid treasures: [5]Then shalt thou understand the fear of Jehovah, And find the knowledge of God. [6] For

Jehovah giveth wisdom; Out of his mouth cometh knowledge and understanding: [7] He layeth up sound wisdom for the upright; He is a shield to them that walk in integrity; [8] That he may guard the paths of justice, And preserve the way of his saints. [9] Then shalt thou understand righteousness and justice, And equity, yea, every good path. [10] For wisdom shall enter into thy heart, And knowledge shall be pleasant unto thy soul; [11] Discretion shall watch over thee; Understanding shall keep thee: [12] To deliver thee from the way of evil, From the men that speak perverse things; [13] Who forsake the paths of uprightness, To walk in the ways of darkness; [14] Who rejoice to do evil, And delight in the perverseness of evil; [15] Who are crooked in their ways, And wayward in their paths: [16] To deliver thee from the strange woman, Even from the foreigner that flattereth with her words; [17] That forsaketh the friend of her youth, And forgetteth the covenant of her God: [18] For her house inclineth unto death, And her paths unto the dead; [19] None that go unto her return again, Neither do they attain unto the paths of life: [20] That thou mayest walk in the way of good men, And keep the paths of the righteous. [21] For the upright shall dwell in the land, And the perfect shall remain in it. [22] But the wicked shall be cut off from the land, And the treacherous shall be rooted out of it.

Reading Plan:

☐ **Proverbs 3 – Trust in the Lord**

3 [1] My son, forget not my law; But let thy heart keep my commandments: [2] For length of days, and years of life, And peace, will they add to thee. [3] Let not kindness and truth forsake thee: Bind them about thy neck; Write them upon the tablet of thy heart: [4] So shalt thou find favor and good understanding In the sight of God and man. [5] Trust in Jehovah with all thy heart, And lean not upon thine own understanding: [6] In all thy ways acknowledge him, And he will direct thy paths. [7] Be not wise in thine own eyes; Fear Jehovah, and depart from evil: [8] It will be health to thy navel, And marrow to thy bones. [9] Honor

Jehovah with thy substance, And with the first-fruits of all thine increase: [10] So shall thy barns be filled with plenty, And thy vats shall overflow with new wine. [11]My son, despise not the chastening of Jehovah; Neither be weary of his reproof: [12] For whom Jehovah loveth he reproveth, Even as a father the son in whom he delighteth. [13] Happy is the man that findeth wisdom, And the man that getteth understanding. [14] For the gaining of it is better than the gaining of silver, And the profit thereof than fine gold. [15] She is more precious than rubies: And none of the things thou canst desire are to be compared unto her. [16] Length of days is in her right hand; In her left hand are riches and honor. [17] Her ways are ways of pleasantness, And all her paths are peace. [18] She is a tree of life to them that lay hold upon her: And happy is every one that retaineth her. [19] Jehovah by wisdom founded the earth; By understanding he established the heavens. [20] By his knowledge the depths were broken up, And the skies drop down the dew. [21]My son, let them not depart from thine eyes; Keep sound wisdom and discretion: [22] So shall they be life unto thy soul, And grace to thy neck. [23] Then shalt thou walk in thy way securely, And thy foot shall not stumble. [24]When thou liest down, thou shalt not be afraid: Yea, thou shalt lie down, and thy sleep shall be sweet. [25]Be not afraid of sudden fear, Neither of the desolation of the wicked, when it cometh: [26] For Jehovah will be thy confidence, And will keep thy foot from being taken. [27]Withhold not good from them to whom it is due, When it is in the power of thy hand to do it. [28] Say not unto thy neighbor, Go, and come again, And to-morrow I will give; When thou hast it by thee. [29]Devise not evil against thy neighbor, Seeing he dwelleth securely by thee. [30] Strive not with a man without cause, If he have done thee no harm. [31]Envy thou not the man of violence, And choose none of his ways. [32] For the perverse is an abomination to Jehovah; But his friendship is with the upright. [33] The curse of Jehovah is in the house of the wicked; But he blesseth the habitation of the righteous. [34] Surely he scoffeth at the scoffers; But he giveth grace unto the lowly. [35]The wise shall inherit glory; But shame shall be the promotion of fools.

Teaching & Commentary

Proverbs 1 – The Purpose of Proverbs & Warning Against Enticement

Imagine sitting down, across from Solomon. He begins, "I want you to enjoy life. Hear me out." He goes on to say, wisdom begins with honoring and revering God more than anything else.

In our culture today, we're bombarded in every direction. We are told to "follow our hearts," or "listen to our gut instincts," but Proverbs teaches us that our hearts need to be ordered. Wisdom does not begin with self; it begins with God.

Proverbs 2 – The Value of Wisdom

Solomon compares wisdom to treasure. We may stumble upon hidden treasure or come across a forgotten diamond wedding band. But wisdom does not just appear, it's something we must search for by being teachable, digging deep, and asking God to provide us with insight.

Perhaps you may have found yourself feeling impatient at times. We want all the answers to questions or situations - right now! Spiritual wisdom is not something that happens overnight; it takes time for deep spiritual roots to grow. However, if we know enough to value wisdom and trust in God, he tells us to ask and he will generously give it!

Proverbs 3 – Trust in the Lord

Some of the Bible's most consoling promises can be found in these passages. Although it may seem simple to put all our trust in the Lord, we tend to cling to our conception of life when things get difficult. God says: "Let me lead you, what you cannot see, I can see."

When we trust God, we let go of our plans and believe that everything will work out for the best. God will provide us with peace and guidance that we cannot find anywhere else, but we must abandon our plans and put our faith in him.

Bottom Line:

Wisdom begins when we put God in His rightful place—above our opinions, our plans, and our understanding. When we acknowledge Him, appreciate His truth as a treasure we are searching out, and offer Him our heart, we will find the direction and peace we have been longing for.

Let's Talk Abouts It

1. What does "the fear of the Lord" mean to you personally?

2. Why do you think wisdom is compared to hidden treasure?

3. Where are you tempted to lean on your own understanding instead of trusting God?

4. What's one area of your life you want to surrender to God this week?

Apply It to Your Life

- **Day 1:** Reflect on areas where you've been relying on yourself more than God.

- **Day 2:** Write Proverbs 1:7 on a card and keep it where you'll see it.

- **Day 3:** Pray for wisdom about something you're facing right now.

- **Day 4:** Think about one decision you can trust God with instead of worrying.

Think About It & Do It

- **Wisdom Journal:** Each day, write down one thing you learned about wisdom or trusting God.

- **Verse Meditation:** Spend 5 minutes quietly repeating Proverbs 1:7.

- **Heart Check:** At the end of the week, ask: *Did I trust God or lean on myself?*

Memory Verse

"The fear of the LORD is the beginning of knowledge, but fools despise wisdom and instruction."
- Proverbs 1:7

📓 It's time to Journal!

Reflect on how this week's teaching speaks to your current season of life. Now write it down.

Let's Pray

Lord, thank You for being the source of all wisdom. Teach me to trust You more than myself. Show me how to respect You in everything I do. Help me walk in Your ways this week and always.

In Jesus' name, Amen.

Week 2: Guarding Your Heart

Theme: Walking the Path of Righteousness
Weekly Focus: Proverbs 4–6

Let's Pray

Father God, thank You for caring so much about my heart. This week, help me see what influences are shaping my thoughts and choices. Give me wisdom to guard my heart and walk in Your ways.

In Jesus' name, Amen.

Reading Plan:

☐ **Proverbs 4 – A Father's Wisdom & Guarding the Heart**

4 [1] Hear, my sons, the instruction of a father, And attend to know understanding: [2] For I give you good doctrine; Forsake ye not my law. [3] For I was a son unto my father, Tender and only beloved in the sight of my mother. [4]And he taught me, and said unto me: Let thy heart retain my words; Keep my commandments, and live; [5]Get wisdom, get understanding; Forget not, neither decline from the words of my mouth; [6] Forsake her not, and she will preserve thee; Love her, and she will keep thee. [7]Wisdom is the principal thing; therefore get wisdom; Yea, with all thy getting get understanding. [8] Exalt her, and she will promote thee; She will bring thee to honor, when thou dost embrace her. [9] She will give to thy head a chaplet of grace; A crown of beauty will she deliver to thee. [10] Hear, O my son, and receive my sayings; And the years of thy life shall be many. [11] I have taught thee in the way of wisdom; I have led thee in paths of uprightness. [12]When thou goest, thy steps shall not be straitened; And if thou runnest, thou shalt not stumble. [13] Take fast hold of instruction; let her not go: Keep her; for she is thy life. [14]Enter not into the path of the wicked, And walk not in the way of evil men. [15]Avoid it, pass not by it; Turn from it, and pass on. 16 For they sleep not, except

19

they do evil; And their sleep is taken away, unless they cause some to fall. 17For they eat the bread of wickedness, And drink the wine of violence. 18 But the path of the righteous is as the dawning light, That shineth more and more unto the perfect day. 19 The way of the wicked is as darkness: They know not at what they stumble. 20My son, attend to my words; Incline thine ear unto my sayings. 21Let them not depart from thine eyes; Keep them in the midst of thy heart. 22 For they are life unto those that find them, And health to all their flesh. 23Keep thy heart with all diligence; For out of it are the issues of life. 24 Put away from thee a wayward mouth, And perverse lips put far from thee. 25Let thine eyes look right on, And let thine eyelids look straight before thee. 26Make level the path of thy feet, And let all thy ways be established. 27Turn not to the right hand nor to the left: Remove thy foot from evil.

Reading Plan:

☐ **Proverbs 5 – Warning Against Adultery**

5 ¹My son, attend unto my wisdom; Incline thine ear to my understanding: ² That thou mayest preserve discretion, And that thy lips may keep knowledge. ³ For the lips of a strange woman drop honey, And her mouth is smoother than oil: ⁴But in the end she is bitter as wormwood, Sharp as a two-edged sword. ⁵ Her feet go down to death; Her steps take hold on Sheol; ⁶ So that she findeth not the level path of life: Her ways are unstable, and she knoweth it not. ⁷Now therefore, my sons, hearken unto me, And depart not from the words of my mouth. ⁸Remove thy way far from her, And come not nigh the door of her house; ⁹Lest thou give thine honor unto others, And thy years unto the cruel; ¹⁰Lest strangers be filled with thy strength, And thy labors be in the house of an alien, ¹¹And thou mourn at thy latter end, When thy flesh and thy body are consumed, ¹²And say, How have I hated instruction, And my heart despised reproof; ¹³Neither have I obeyed the voice of my teachers, Nor inclined mine ear to them that instructed me! ¹⁴ I was well-nigh in all evil In the midst of the assembly and congregation. ¹⁵Drink

waters out of thine own cistern, And running waters out of thine own well. [16] Should thy springs be dispersed abroad, And streams of water in the streets? [17]Let them be for thyself alone, And not for strangers with thee. [18] Let thy fountain be blessed; And rejoice in the wife of thy youth. [19]As a loving hind and a pleasant doe, Let her breasts satisfy thee at all times; And be thou ravished always with her love. [20] For why shouldest thou, my son, be ravished with a strange woman, And embrace the bosom of a foreigner? [21]For the ways of man are before the eyes of Jehovah; And he maketh level all his paths. [22] His own iniquities shall take the wicked, And he shall be holden with the cords of his sin. [23] He shall die for lack of instruction; And in the greatness of his folly he shall go astray.

Reading Plan:

☐ **Proverbs 6 – Warnings Against Folly and Wickedness**

6[1]My son, if thou art become surety for thy neighbor, If thou hast stricken thy hands for a stranger; [2] Thou art snared with the words of thy mouth, Thou art taken with the words of thy mouth. [3]Do this now, my son, and deliver thyself, Seeing thou art come into the hand of thy neighbor: Go, humble thyself, and importune thy neighbor; [4]Give not sleep to thine eyes, Nor slumber to thine eyelids; [5]Deliver thyself as a roe from the hand of the hunter, And as a bird from the hand of the fowler. [6]Go to the ant, thou sluggard; Consider her ways, and be wise: [7]Which having no chief, Overseer, or ruler, [8] Provideth her bread in the summer, And gathereth her food in the harvest. [9] How long wilt thou sleep, O sluggard? When wilt thou arise out of thy sleep? [10] Yet a little sleep, a little slumber, A little folding of the hands to sleep: [11]So shall thy poverty come as a robber, And thy want as an armed man. [12]A worthless person, a man of iniquity, Is he that walketh with a perverse mouth; [13] That winketh with his eyes, that speaketh with his feet, That maketh signs with his fingers; [14] In whose heart is perverseness, Who deviseth evil continually, Who soweth discord. [15]Therefore shall his calamity come suddenly; On a sudden shall he be broken, and that without remedy. [16] There are six things which Jehovah hateth; Yea, seven which are an abomination unto him: [17] Haughty eyes, a lying tongue, And hands that shed innocent blood; [18] A heart that deviseth wicked purposes, Feet that are swift in running to mischief, [19]A false witness that uttereth lies, And he that soweth discord among brethren. [20]My son, keep the commandment of thy father, And forsake not the law of thy mother: [21]Bind them continually upon thy heart; Tie them about thy neck. [22]When thou walkest, it shall lead thee; When thou sleepest, it shall watch over thee; And when thou awakest, it shall talk with thee. [23] For the commandment is a lamp; and the law is light; And reproofs of instruction are the way of life: [24] To keep thee from the evil woman, From the flattery of the foreigner's tongue. [25]Lust not after her beauty in thy heart; Neither let her take thee with her eyelids. [26] For on account of a harlot a man is brought to a piece of bread; And the adulteress hunteth for the precious life. [27]Can a man take fire in his bosom, And his clothes not be burned? [28]Or can one walk upon hot coals, And his feet not be scorched? [29] So he that goeth in to his neighbor's wife; Whosoever toucheth her shall not be unpunished. [30]Men do not despise a thief, if he steal To satisfy himself when he is hungry: [31]But if he be found, he shall restore sevenfold; He shall give all the substance of his house. [32] He that committeth adultery with a woman is void of understanding: He doeth it who would destroy his own soul. [33]Wounds and dishonor shall he get; And his reproach shall not be wiped away. [34] For jealousy is the rage of a man; And he will not spare in the day of vengeance. [35] He will not regard any ransom; Neither will he rest content, though thou givest many gifts.

Teaching & Commentary

Proverbs 4 – A Father's Wisdom & Guarding the Heart

Solomon seems to have the foresight of a parent. "Hear me out: your heart is your greatest asset," he says.

There is a lot of competition for our affection in the world we live in, including social media, entertainment, and other people's viewpoints. According to Proverbs 4, everything in our life originates from our hearts. We will discover our path if we allow God's truth to fill our heart. We will make bad choices and say terrible things if we don't protect our heart.

Here are some examples of what it looks like to protect our hearts in today's climate:

- Limiting critical voices on the internet
- Choosing music, shows, and friendships that align with your faith.
- And making time daily for God's Word

Proverbs 5 – Warning Against Adultery

This chapter is very straightforward—Solomon doesn't dance around the subject of sexual temptation. He declares that it may look sweet and innocent, but it leads only to pain and suffering.

In our culture, sin, adultery, and sexual infidelity look normal or exciting. But God's wisdom is still the same: protect your relationships and your integrity. Even if you are single, it is about practicing self-control and showing God that we honor Him with our bodies and our choices.

Some practical applications may include:

- Setting healthy boundaries with co-workers or friends
- Setting filters or accountability apps to your devices
- Avoiding entertainment that leaves to temptation.

Proverbs 6 – Warnings Against Folly and Wickedness

This chapter covered a lot of territory:

• Laziness... Solomon says, "Look at the ant—she doesn't require someone watching over her to get things done." Today, procrastination has become a widespread problem. God values diligence and faithfulness in the trivial things.

• Dishonesty & Dramatizing.... God hates lies, hearsay, and discord. Little lies matter and can destroy trust. With the ease of posting and sharing, we need to be careful with our words, leave the drama to the movies! Proverbs remind us to guard our words carefully.

• Adultery Again.... Solomon brings this same warning because unfaithful hearts destroy lives. Adultery isn't only a physical act; it begins in the heart.

Bottom Line:

We can't just think it's a one-time thing to guard our hearts; it's a choice we must make every single day. When we protect what we allow into our hearts we not only honor God, but we also protect our integrity, relationships, and as well we continue to grow in wisdom.

Let's Talk About It

1. What does it mean to "guard your heart" in your daily life?

2. Which of these warnings feels most relevant to you right now?

3. Where do you see the culture's messages about sex and relationships clashing with God's wisdom?

4. What boundaries could help you stay on the right path?

Apply It to Your Life

• **Day 1:** Reflect on what influences you've allowed into your heart.

- **Day 2:** Write down practical ways to protect your heart this week.

- **Day 3:** Pray for strength to resist temptation and stay focused on God.

- **Day 4:** Choose one positive habit to replace something harmful.

Think About It & Do It

- **Heart Check:** Each night, ask, *what did I let into my heart today?*

- **Verse Meditation:** Spend 5 minutes quietly repeating Proverbs 4:23.

- **Wisdom Journal:** Write down one way you guarded your heart each day.

Memory Verse

"Above all else, guard your heart, for everything you do flows from it."
*- **Proverbs 4:23***

📖 It's time to Journal!

Reflect on how this week's teaching speaks to your current season of life. Now write it down.

Let's Pray

Lord, thank You for reminding me how much my heart matters. Help me guard it with wisdom, courage, and grace. Show me anything I need to change and give me strength to walk in purity and truth.

In Jesus' name, Amen

Week 3: Wisdom Versus Folly

Theme: Choosing the Way of Wisdom
Weekly Focus: Proverbs 7–9

Let's Pray

Father God, thank You for showing me the difference between wisdom and foolishness. Help me clearly see the paths before me and give me courage to choose what honors You. Guard my heart and mind this week.

In Jesus' name, Amen.

Reading Plan:

☐ **Proverbs 7 – Warning Against the Adulterer**

7 [1]My son, keep my words, And lay up my commandments with thee. [2]Keep my commandments and live; And my law as the apple of thine eye. [3]Bind them upon thy fingers; Write them upon the tablet of thy heart. [4] Say unto wisdom, Thou art my sister; And call understanding thy kinswoman: [5]That they may keep thee from the strange woman, From the foreigner that flattereth with her words. [6] For at the window of my house I looked forth through my lattice; [7]And I beheld among the simple ones, I discerned among the youths, A young man void of understanding, [8] Passing through the street near her corner; And he went the way to her house, [9] In the twilight, in the evening of the day, In the middle of the night and in the darkness. [10] And, behold, there met him a woman With the attire of a harlot, and wily of heart. [11] (She is clamorous and wilful; Her feet abide not in her house: [12]Now she is in the streets, now in the broad places, And lieth in wait at every corner.) [13] So she caught him, and kissed him, And with an impudent face she said unto him: [14] Sacrifices of peace-offerings are with me; This day have I paid my vows. [15]Therefore came I forth to meet thee, Diligently to seek thy face, and I have found thee. [16] I have spread my couch with carpets of tapestry, With striped cloths of the yarn of Egypt. [17] I have perfumed my bed With

myrrh, aloes, and cinnamon. [18] Come, let us take our fill of love until the morning; Let us solace ourselves with loves. [19] For the man is not at home; He is gone a long journey: [20] He hath taken a bag of money with him; He will come home at the full moon. [21]With her much fair speech she causeth him to yield; With the flattering of her lips she forceth him along. [22] He goeth after her straightway, As an ox goeth to the slaughter, Or as one in fetters to the correction of the fool; [23] Till an arrow strike through his liver; As a bird hasteth to the snare, And knoweth not that it is for his life. [24]Now therefore, my sons, hearken unto me, And attend to the words of my mouth. [25]Let not thy heart decline to her ways; Go not astray in her paths. [26] For she hath cast down many wounded: Yea, all her slain are a mighty host. [27] Her house is the way to Sheol, Going down to the chambers of death.

Reading Plan:

☐ Proverbs 8 – The Call of Wisdom

8 [1]Doth not wisdom cry, And understanding put forth her voice? [2]On the top of high places by the way, Where the paths meet, she standeth; [3]Beside the gates, at the entry of the city, At the coming in at the doors, she crieth aloud: [4]Unto you, O men, I call; And my voice is to the sons of men. [5]O ye simple, understand prudence; And, ye fools, be of an understanding heart. [6] Hear, for I will speak excellent things; And the opening of my lips shall be right things. [7]For my mouth shall utter truth; And wickedness is an abomination to my lips. [8] All the words of my mouth are in righteousness; There is nothing crooked or perverse in them. [9] They are all plain to him that understandeth, And right to them that find knowledge. [10]Receive my instruction, and not silver; And knowledge rather than choice gold. [11]For wisdom is better than rubies; And all the things that may be desired are not to be compared unto it. [12] I wisdom have made prudence my dwelling, And find out knowledge and discretion. [13] The fear of Jehovah is to hate evil: Pride, and arrogancy, and the evil way, And the perverse mouth, do I hate. [14] Counsel is mine, and

sound knowledge: I am understanding; I have might. ¹⁵By me kings reign, And princes decree justice. ¹⁶By me princes rule, And nobles, even all the judges of the earth. ¹⁷ I love them that love me; And those that seek me diligently shall find me. ¹⁸Riches and honor are with me; Yea, durable wealth and righteousness. ¹⁹My fruit is better than gold, yea, than fine gold; And my revenue than choice silver. ²⁰ I walk in the way of righteousness, In the midst of the paths of justice; ²¹That I may cause those that love me to inherit substance, And that I may fill their treasuries. ²² Jehovah possessed me in the beginning of his way, Before his works of old. ²³ I was set up from everlasting, from the beginning, Before the earth was. ²⁴When there were no depths, I was brought forth, When there were no fountains abounding with water. ²⁵Before the mountains were settled, Before the hills was I brought forth; ²⁶While as yet he had not made the earth, nor the fields, Nor the beginning of the dust of the world. ²⁷When he established the heavens, I was there: When he set a circle upon the face of the deep, ²⁸When he made firm the skies above, When the fountains of the deep became strong, ²⁹When he gave to the sea its bound, That the waters should not transgress his commandment, When he marked out the foundations of the earth; ³⁰ Then I was by him, as a master workman; And I was daily his delight, Rejoicing always before him, ³¹Rejoicing in his habitable earth; And my delight was with the sons of men. ³²Now therefore, my sons, hearken unto me; For blessed are they that keep my ways. ³³ Hear instruction, and be wise, And refuse it not. ³⁴Blessed is the man that heareth me, Watching daily at my gates, Waiting at the posts of my doors. ³⁵ For whoso findeth me findeth life, And shall obtain favor of Jehovah. ³⁶But he that sinneth against me wrongeth his own soul: All they that hate me love death.

Reading Plan:

☐ **Proverbs 9 – Invitations of Wisdom and Folly**

9 ¹Wisdom hath builded her house; She hath hewn out her seven pillars: ² She hath killed her beasts; she hath mingled her wine; She hath also furnished her table: ³ She hath sent forth her maidens; She crieth upon the highest places of the city: ⁴Whoso is simple, let him turn in hither: As for him that is void of understanding, she saith to him, ⁵Come, eat ye of my bread, And drink of the wine which I have mingled. ⁶ Leave off, ye simple ones, and live; And walk in the way of understanding. ⁷ He that correcteth a scoffer getteth to himself reviling; And he that reproveth a wicked man getteth himself a blot. ⁸Reprove not a scoffer, lest he hate thee: Reprove a wise man, and he will love thee. ⁹Give instruction to a wise man, and he will be yet wiser: Teach a righteous man, and he will increase in learning. ¹⁰ The fear of Jehovah is the beginning of wisdom; And the knowledge of the Holy One is understanding. ¹¹For by me thy days shall be multiplied, And the years of thy life shall be increased. ¹² If thou art wise, thou art wise for thyself; And if thou scoffest, thou alone shalt bear it. ¹³ The foolish woman is clamorous; She is simple, and knoweth nothing. ¹⁴And she sitteth at the door of her house, On a seat in the high places of the city, ¹⁵To call to them that pass by, Who go right on their ways: ¹⁶Whoso is simple, let him turn in hither; And as for him that is void of understanding, she saith to him, ¹⁷Stolen waters are sweet, And bread eaten in secret is pleasant. ¹⁸ But he knoweth not that the dead are there; That her guests are in the depths of Sheol.

Teaching & Commentary

Proverbs 7 – Warning Against the Adulteress

This chapter reads like a colorful story. Solomon begins with a description of a young man walking into temptation. He is oblivious, unprepared, and trapped.

Today, temptation is not always easy to identify. Things may seem harmless, such as flirting, or there may be a secret habit no one knows about. Proverbs 7 reminds us that temptation often feels thrilling when it occurs but always ends in distress. God calls us to be alert and wise about the choices we are making.

Proverbs 8 – The Call of Wisdom

In Proverbs 8, wisdom itself is speaking to us, calling out in the streets, offering knowledge and understanding to whoever takes time to listen. Wisdom exclaims, "I have counsel, I have insight, and I have strength. Blessed are those who love me."

Today, God still offers us His wisdom. However, we must allow ourselves to slow down long enough to hear His voice above the noise of everything else. Seeking wisdom in our lives is intentionally taking daily time to read Scripture, asking God for direction in life, and surrounding ourselves with friends who will speak truth into our lives.

Proverbs 9 – Invitations of Wisdom and Folly

It's clear: there are two invitations available. The first is from Wisdom - she provides life, knowledge, and satisfaction of soul. The other is from Folly -she offers stolen pleasures, which lead to death.

Every day we have a choice. Are we going to take the invitation from God, or the invitation from the world? Will we build a life based on truth or chase the best feelings in the moment?

Bottom Line:

Wisdom and foolishness are both calling you. Every day you choose which voice you will hear. And in choosing wisdom, you choose life, peace, and the blessing of God.

Let's Talk About It

1. What stands out to you about the way temptation is described in Proverbs 7?

2. How do you recognize God's wisdom calling you in your daily life?

3. Why do you think it's so easy to choose what feels good in the moment over what's truly wise?

4. What can help you listen to wisdom instead of folly?

Apply It to Your Life

- **Day 1:** Reflect on areas where you're most tempted to compromise.

- **Day 2:** Spend 10 minutes reading Proverbs 8 slowly, imagining Wisdom speaking directly to you.

- **Day 3:** Write down one decision where you need God's wisdom right now.

- **Day 4:** Ask a trusted friend or mentor to pray with you about walking in wisdom.

Think About It & Do It

- **Wisdom Journal:** Write down one wise choice you made each day.

- **Verse Meditation:** Spend 5 minutes quietly repeating Proverbs 9:10.

- **Heart Check:** Before bed, ask yourself: *Which voice did I follow today?*

Memory Verse

"The fear of the LORD is the beginning of wisdom, and knowledge of the Holy One is understanding."
- Proverbs 9:10

📓 It's time to Journal!

Reflect on how this week's teaching speaks to your current season of life. Now write it down.

Let's Pray

Lord, thank You for offering me Your wisdom so freely. Help me to hear Your voice above every distraction. Give me strength to walk away from foolish choices and follow You with all my heart.

In Jesus' name, Amen.

Week 4: Living with Integrity

Theme: The Ways of the Upright
Weekly Focus: Proverbs 10–14

Let's Pray

Father God, thank You for showing me how important integrity is. Teach me to be honest in everything I do. Help me to reflect Your character in my words, my choices, and my relationships.

In Jesus' name, Amen.

Reading Plan:

☐ **Proverbs 10 – Proverbs of Solomon: Wise and Foolish Conduct**

10 [1]The proverbs of Solomon. A wise son maketh a glad father; But a foolish son is the heaviness of his mother. [2] Treasures of wickedness profit nothing; But righteousness delivereth from death. [3] Jehovah will not suffer the soul of the righteous to famish; But he thrusteth away the desire of the wicked. [4] He becometh poor that worketh with a slack hand; But the hand of the diligent maketh rich. [5] He that gathereth in summer is a wise son; But he that sleepeth in harvest is a son that causeth shame. [6]Blessings are upon the head of the righteous; But violence covereth the mouth of the wicked. [7]The memory of the righteous is blessed; But the name of the wicked shall rot. [8] The wise in heart will receive commandments; But a prating fool shall fall. [9] He that walketh uprightly walketh surely; But he that perverteth his ways shall be known. [10] He that winketh with the eye causeth sorrow; But a prating fool shall fall. [11]The mouth of the righteous is a fountain of life; But violence covereth the mouth of the wicked. [12] Hatred stirreth up strifes; But love covereth all transgressions. [13] In the lips of him that hath discernment wisdom is found; But a rod is for the back of him that is void of understanding. [14]Wise men lay up knowledge; But the mouth of the foolish is a present destruction. [15]The rich man's wealth is his strong city:

The destruction of the poor is their poverty. [16] The labor of the righteous tendeth to life; The increase of the wicked, to sin. [17] He is in the way of life that heedeth correction; But he that forsaketh reproof erreth. [18] He that hideth hatred is of lying lips; And he that uttereth a slander is a fool. [19] In the multitude of words there wanteth not transgression; But he that refraineth his lips doeth wisely. [20] The tongue of the righteous is as choice silver: The heart of the wicked is little worth. [21]The lips of the righteous feed many; But the foolish die for lack of understanding. [22] The blessing of Jehovah, it maketh rich; And he addeth no sorrow therewith. [23] It is as sport to a fool to do wickedness; And so is wisdom to a man of understanding. [24] The fear of the wicked, it shall come upon him; And the desire of the righteous shall be granted. [25]When the whirlwind passeth, the wicked is no more; But the righteous is an everlasting foundation. [26]As vinegar to the teeth, and as smoke to the eyes, So is the sluggard to them that send him. [27]The fear of Jehovah prolongeth days; But the years of the wicked shall be shortened. [28] The hope of the righteous shall be gladness; But the expectation of the wicked shall perish. [29] The way of Jehovah is a stronghold to the upright; But it is a destruction to the workers of iniquity. [30] The righteous shall never be removed; But the wicked shall not dwell in the land. [31]The mouth of the righteous bringeth forth wisdom; But the perverse tongue shall be cut off. [32] The lips of the righteous know what is acceptable; But the mouth of the wicked speaketh perverseness.

Reading Plan:

☐ **Proverbs 11 – Righteousness and Integrity**

11
[1]A false balance is an abomination to Jehovah; But a just weight is his delight. [2]When pride cometh, then cometh shame; But with the lowly is wisdom. [3] The integrity of the upright shall guide them; But the perverseness of the treacherous shall destroy them. [4]Riches profit not in the day of wrath; But righteousness delivereth from death. [5]The righteousness of the perfect shall direct his

way; But the wicked shall fall by his own wickedness. [6] The righteousness of the upright shall deliver them; But the treacherous shall be taken in their own iniquity. [7]When a wicked man dieth, his expectation shall perish; And the hope of iniquity perisheth. [8] The righteous is delivered out of trouble; And the wicked cometh in his stead. [9]With his mouth the godless man destroyeth his neighbor; But through knowledge shall the righteous be delivered. [10]When it goeth well with the righteous, the city rejoiceth; And when the wicked perish, there is shouting. [11]By the blessing of the upright the city is exalted; But it is overthrown by the mouth of the wicked. [12] He that despiseth his neighbor is void of wisdom; But a man of understanding holdeth his peace. [13] He that goeth about as a tale-bearer revealeth secrets; But he that is of a faithful spirit concealeth a matter. [14]Where no wise guidance is, the people falleth; But in the multitude of counsellors there is safety. [15] He that is surety for a stranger shall smart for it; But he that hateth suretyship is secure. [16]A gracious woman obtaineth honor; And violent men obtain riches. [17]The merciful man doeth good to his own soul; But he that is cruel troubleth his own flesh. [18] The wicked earneth deceitful wages; But he that soweth righteousness hath a sure reward. [19] He that is stedfast in righteousness shall attain unto life; And he that pursueth evil doeth it to his own death. [20] They that are perverse in heart are an abomination to Jehovah; But such as are perfect in their way are his delight. [21]Though hand join in hand, the evil man shall not be unpunished; But the seed of the righteous shall be delivered. [22]As a ring of gold in a swine's snout, So is a fair woman that is without discretion. [23] The desire of the righteous is only good; But the expectation of the wicked is wrath. [24] There is that scattereth, and increaseth yet more; And there is that withholdeth more than is meet, but it tendeth only to want. [25]The liberal soul shall be made fat; And he that watereth shall be watered also himself. [26] He that withholdeth grain, the people shall curse him; But blessing shall be upon the head of him that selleth it. [27] He that diligently seeketh good seeketh favor; But he that searcheth after evil, it shall come unto him. [28] He that trusteth in his riches shall fall; But the righteous shall flourish as the green leaf. [29] He that troubleth his own house shall inherit the wind; And the foolish shall be servant to the wise of heart. ³⁰ The fruit of the righteous is a tree of life; And he that is wise winneth souls. ³¹Behold, the righteous shall be recompensed in the earth; How much more the wicked and the sinner!

Reading Plan:

☐ Proverbs 12 – Loving Discipline and Goodness

12 ¹Whoso loveth correction loveth knowledge; But he that hateth reproof is brutish. ²A good man shall obtain favor of Jehovah; But a man of wicked devices will he condemn. ³A man shall not be established by wickedness; But the root of the righteous shall not be moved. ⁴A worthy woman is the crown of her husband; But she that maketh ashamed is as rottenness in his bones. ⁵The thoughts of the righteous are just; But the counsels of the wicked are deceit. ⁶ The words of the wicked are of lying in wait for blood; But the mouth of the upright shall deliver them. ⁷The wicked are overthrown, and are not; But the house of the righteous shall stand. ⁸ A man shall be commended according to his wisdom; But he that is of a perverse heart shall be despised. ⁹Better is he that is lightly esteemed, and hath a servant, Than he that honoreth himself, and lacketh bread. ¹⁰ A righteous man regardeth the life of his beast; But the tender mercies of the wicked are cruel. ¹¹ He that tilleth his land shall have plenty of bread; But he that followeth after vain persons is void of understanding. ¹² The wicked desireth the net of evil men; But the root of the righteous yieldeth fruit. ¹³ In the transgression of the lips is a snare to the evil man; But the righteous shall come out of trouble. ¹⁴A man shall be satisfied with good by the fruit of his mouth; And the doings of a man's hands shall be rendered unto him. ¹⁵The way of a fool is right in his own eyes; But he that is wise hearkeneth unto counsel. ¹⁶A fool's vexation is presently known; But a prudent man concealeth shame. ¹⁷ He that uttereth truth showeth forth righteousness; But a false witness, deceit. ¹⁸ There is that speaketh rashly like the piercings of a sword; But the tongue of the wise

is health. [19] The lip of truth shall be established for ever; But a lying tongue is but for a moment. [20]Deceit is in the heart of them that devise evil; But to the counsellors of peace is joy. [21]There shall no mischief happen to the righteous; But the wicked shall be filled with evil. [22] Lying lips are an abomination to Jehovah; But they that deal truly are his delight. [23]A prudent man concealeth knowledge; But the heart of fools proclaimeth foolishness. [24] The hand of the diligent shall bear rule; But the slothful shall be put under taskwork. [25] Heaviness in the heart of a man maketh it stoop; But a good word maketh it glad. [26] The righteous is a guide to his neighbor; But the way of the wicked causeth them to err. [27]The slothful man roasteth not that which he took in hunting; But the precious substance of men is to the diligent. [28] In the way of righteousness is life; And in the pathway thereof there is no death.

Reading Plan:

☐ Proverbs 13 – Wise Living and Diligence

13 [1]A wise son heareth his father's instruction; But a scoffer heareth not rebuke. [2]A man shall eat good by the fruit of his mouth; But the soul of the treacherous shall eat violence. [3] He that guardeth his mouth keepeth his life; But he that openeth wide his lips shall have destruction. [4] The soul of the sluggard desireth, and hath nothing; But the soul of the diligent shall be made fat. [5]A righteous man hateth lying; But a wicked man is loathsome, and cometh to shame. [6]Righteousness guardeth him that is upright in the way; But wickedness overthroweth the sinner. [7]There is that maketh himself rich, yet hath nothing: There is that maketh himself poor, yet hath great wealth. [8] The ransom of a man's life is his riches; But the poor heareth no threatening. [9] The light of the righteous rejoiceth; But the lamp of the wicked shall be put out. [10] By pride cometh only contention; But with the well-advised is wisdom. [11]Wealth gotten by vanity shall be diminished; But he that gathereth by labor shall have increase. [12] Hope deferred maketh the heart sick; But when the desire cometh, it is a tree of life. [13]Whoso despiseth the word bringeth destruction on himself; But he that feareth the commandment shall be rewarded. ¹⁴ The law of the wise is a fountain of life, That one may depart from the snares of death. ¹⁵Good understanding giveth favor; But the way of the transgressor is hard. ¹⁶Every prudent man worketh with knowledge; But a fool flaunteth his folly. ¹⁷A wicked messenger falleth into evil; But a faithful ambassador is health. ¹⁸ Poverty and shame shall be to him that refuseth correction; But he that regardeth reproof shall be honored. ¹⁹ The desire accomplished is sweet to the soul; But it is an abomination to fools to depart from evil. ²⁰Walk with wise men, and thou shalt be wise; But the companion of fools shall smart for it. ²¹Evil pursueth sinners; But the righteous shall be recompensed with good. ²²A good man leaveth an inheritance to his children's children; And the wealth of the sinner is laid up for the righteous. ²³Much food is in the tillage of the poor; But there is that is destroyed by reason of injustice. ²⁴ He that spareth his rod hateth his son; But he that loveth him chasteneth him betimes. ²⁵The righteous eateth to the satisfying of his soul; But the belly of the wicked shall want.

Reading Plan:

☐ Proverbs 14 – The Upright and the Fool

14 ¹Every wise woman buildeth her house; But the foolish plucketh it down with her own hands. ² He that walketh in his uprightness feareth Jehovah; But he that is perverse in his ways despiseth him. ³ In the mouth of the foolish is a rod for his pride; But the lips of the wise shall preserve them. ⁴Where no oxen are, the crib is clean; But much increase is by the strength of the ox. ⁵A faithful witness will not lie; But a false witness uttereth lies. ⁶A scoffer seeketh wisdom, and findeth it not; But knowledge is easy unto him that hath understanding. ⁷Go into the presence of a foolish man, And thou shalt not perceive in him the lips of knowledge. ⁸ The wisdom of the prudent is to understand his way; But the folly of fools is deceit. ⁹A trespass-offering mocketh fools; But among the upright there is good will. ¹⁰ The heart

knoweth its own bitterness; And a stranger doth not intermeddle with its joy. ¹¹The house of the wicked shall be overthrown; But the tent of the upright shall flourish. ¹² There is a way which seemeth right unto a man; But the end thereof are the ways of death. ¹³Even in laughter the heart is sorrowful; And the end of mirth is heaviness. ¹⁴ The backslider in heart shall be filled with his own ways; And a good man shall be satisfied from himself. ¹⁵The simple believeth every word; But the prudent man looketh well to his going. ¹⁶A wise man feareth, and departeth from evil; But the fool beareth himself insolently, and is confident. ¹⁷ He that is soon angry will deal foolishly; And a man of wicked devices is hated. ¹⁸ The simple inherit folly; But the prudent are crowned with knowledge. ¹⁹ The evil bow down before the good; And the wicked, at the gates of the righteous. ²⁰ The poor is hated even of his own neighbor; But the rich hath many friends. ²¹ He that despiseth his neighbor sinneth; But he that hath pity on the poor, happy is he. ²²Do they not err that devise evil? But mercy and truth shall be to them that devise good. ²³ In all labor there is profit; But the talk of the lips tendeth only to penury. ²⁴ The crown of the wise is their riches; But the folly of fools is only folly. ²⁵A true witness delivereth souls; But he that uttereth lies causeth deceit. ²⁶ In the fear of Jehovah is strong confidence; And his children shall have a place of refuge. ²⁷The fear of Jehovah is a fountain of life, That one may depart from the snares of death. ²⁸ In the multitude of people is the king's glory; But in the want of people is the destruction of the prince. ²⁹ He that is slow to anger is of great understanding; But he that is hasty of spirit exalteth folly. ³⁰ A tranquil heart is the life of the flesh; But envy is the rottenness of the bones. ³¹ He that oppresseth the poor reproacheth his Maker; But he that hath mercy on the needy honoreth him. ³² The wicked is thrust down in his evil-doing; But the righteous hath a refuge in his death. ³³Wisdom resteth in the heart of him that hath understanding; But that which is in the inward part of fools is made known. ³⁴Righteousness exalteth a nation; But sin is a reproach to any people. ³⁵The king's favor is toward a servant that dealeth wisely; But his wrath will be against him that causeth shame.

Teaching & Commentary

Proverbs 10 – Wise and Foolish Conduct

In this chapter, Solomon begins a series of many short and pointed sayings (proverbs) that contrast wise and foolish, righteous and wicked, honest and deceitful. It is a reminder that integrity is expressed in our everyday life decisions; the words we speak, the way we work, the way we treat people.

It is possible today to take shortcuts or twist the truth to get ahead. The contrast in Proverbs 10 teaches us that integrity will lead to safety and security, but dishonesty will catch up to us and ultimately lead to our downfall.

Proverbs 11 – Righteousness and Integrity

This chapter looks at the blessings of integrity and the consequences of wickedness. It also focuses on the ripple effect of our conduct on others. When we practice righteous integrity, we bless ourselves and those around us.

God delights in fairness and truth. When we walk in righteousness and integrity, we can trust Him to protect us and bless us.

Proverbs 12 – Loving Discipline and Goodness

Proverbs 12 brings out the specific contrast in the wise versus the fool. Wise people love discipline as it provides correction and growth; fools hate discipline, which leads them astray. This should encourage us to consider humility, this means being humble enough to accept feedback and being willing to change.

Proverbs 13 – Wise Living and Diligence

Solomon emphasizes a key element of discipline and being around good company. "Walk with the wise and become wise, for a companion of fools suffers harm." Who we are around matters. Friends who love God will help our walk as well.

Proverbs 14 – The Upright and the Fool

This chapter continues to contrast wisdom and folly. This chapter mentions a key truth that many times, our very own reasoning can lead to destruction if we are not leaning on God's truth. Solomon also encourages us to be slow to anger, honest in our dealings, and committed to doing what is right, even when no one is watching.

Bottom Line:

Integrity is not just in the large choices you make. Integrity is lived out in the small stuff, day in and day out. Act honestly, work diligently, and humbly accept correction so you can build a life that honors God and blesses others.

Let's Talk About It

1. What does integrity look like in your daily life?

2. Why do you think honesty is so important to God?

3. Who are the people influencing you most right now? Are they helping you walk wisely?

4. What area of your life could use more discipline or honesty?

Apply It to Your Life

- **Day 1:** Reflect on situations where you're tempted to cut corners or hide the truth.

- **Day 2:** Pray for strength to act with integrity even when it's hard.

- **Day 3:** Choose one area where you will practice more discipline this week.

- **Day 4:** Write down the names of people who influence you most and pray for those relationships.

Think About It & Do It

- **Integrity Journal:** Each day, write down one choice you made that reflected honesty.

- **Verse Meditation:** Spend 5 minutes quietly repeating Proverbs 10:9.

- **Heart Check:** Ask yourself before decisions: *Is this honest? Does this honor God?*

Memory Verse

"Whoever walks in integrity walks securely, but whoever takes crooked paths will be found out."
- Proverbs 10:9

📖 It's time to Journal!

Reflect on how this week's teaching speaks to your current season of life. Now write it down.

Let's Pray

Lord, thank You for reminding me of just how much You value integrity. Help me to be honest, diligent, and humble in everything I do. Give me courage to make wise choices even when it's difficult. I want my life to reflect Your truth.

In Jesus' name, Amen.

Keep Going!

God is working in you even when you can't see it. Small steps of obedience lead to lasting change.

Week 5: Wisdom in Relationships

Theme: Honoring God and Others
Weekly Focus: Proverbs 15–19

Let's Pray

Father God, thank You for Your wisdom that guides my relationships. Teach me to honor You in the way I speak, love, and treat others. Help me build healthy connections that reflect Your heart.

In Jesus' name, Amen.

Reading Plan:

☐ **Proverbs 15 – Gentle Answers and Wise Words**

15

^{1}A soft answer turneth away wrath; But a grievous word stirreth up anger. ^{2} The tongue of the wise uttereth knowledge aright; But the mouth of fools poureth out folly. ^{3} The eyes of Jehovah are in every place, Keeping watch upon the evil and the good. ^{4}A gentle tongue is a tree of life; But perverseness therein is a breaking of the spirit. ^{5}A fool despiseth his father's correction; But he that regardeth reproof getteth prudence. ^{6} In the house of the righteous is much treasure; But in the revenues of the wicked is trouble. ^{7}The lips of the wise disperse knowledge; But the heart of the foolish doeth not so. ^{8} The sacrifice of the wicked is an abomination to Jehovah; But the prayer of the upright is his delight. ^{9} The way of the wicked is an abomination to Jehovah; But he loveth him that followeth after righteousness. ^{10} There is grievous correction for him that forsaketh the way; And he that hateth reproof shall die. ^{11}Sheol and Abaddon are before Jehovah; How much more then the hearts of the children of men! ^{12}A scoffer loveth not to be reproved; He will not go unto the wise. ^{13}A glad heart maketh a cheerful countenance; But by sorrow of heart the spirit is broken. ^{14} The heart of him that hath understanding seeketh knowledge; But the mouth of fools feedeth on folly. ¹⁵All the days of the afflicted are evil; But he that is of a cheerful heart hath a continual feast. ¹⁶Better is little, with the fear of Jehovah, Than great treasure and trouble therewith. ¹⁷Better is a dinner of herbs, where love is, Than a stalled ox and hatred therewith. ¹⁸ A wrathful man stirreth up contention; But he that is slow to anger appeaseth strife. ¹⁹ The way of the sluggard is as a hedge of thorns; But the path of the upright is made a highway. ²⁰ A wise son maketh a glad father; But a foolish man despiseth his mother. ²¹Folly is joy to him that is void of wisdom; But a man of understanding maketh straight his going. ²²Where there is no counsel, purposes are disappointed; But in the multitude of counsellors they are established. ²³A man hath joy in the answer of his mouth; And a word in due season, how good is it! ²⁴ To the wise the way of life goeth upward, That he may depart from Sheol beneath. ²⁵ Jehovah will root up the house of the proud; But he will establish the border of the widow. ²⁶Evil devices are an abomination to Jehovah; But pleasant words are pure. ²⁷ He that is greedy of gain troubleth his own house; But he that hateth bribes shall live. ²⁸ The heart of the righteous studieth to answer; But the mouth of the wicked poureth out evil things. ²⁹ Jehovah is far from the wicked; But he heareth the prayer of the righteous. ³⁰ The light of the eyes rejoiceth the heart; And good tidings make the bones fat. ³¹The ear that hearkeneth to the reproof of life Shall abide among the wise. ³² He that refuseth correction despiseth his own soul; But he that hearkeneth to reproof getteth understanding. ³³ The fear of Jehovah is the instruction of wisdom; And before honor goeth humility.

Reading Plan:

□ **Proverbs 16 – Commit Your Plans to the Lord**

16 ¹The plans of the heart belong to man; But the answer of the tongue is from Jehovah. ²All the ways of a man are clean in his own eyes; But Jehovah weigheth the spirits. ³Commit thy works unto Jehovah, And thy purposes shall be established. ⁴ Jehovah

hath made everything for its own end; Yea, even the wicked for the day of evil. [5]Every one that is proud in heart is an abomination to Jehovah: Though hand join in hand, he shall not be unpunished. [6]By mercy and truth iniquity is atoned for; And by the fear of Jehovah men depart from evil. [7]When a man's ways please Jehovah, He maketh even his enemies to be at peace with him. [8] Better is a little, with righteousness, Than great revenues with injustice. [9]A man's heart deviseth his way; But Jehovah directeth his steps. [10] A divine sentence is in the lips of the king; His mouth shall not transgress in judgment. [11]A just balance and scales are Jehovah's; All the weights of the bag are his work. [12] It is an abomination to kings to commit wickedness; For the throne is established by righteousness. [13]Righteous lips are the delight of kings; And they love him that speaketh right. [14] The wrath of a king is as messengers of death; But a wise man will pacify it. [15] In the light of the king's countenance is life; And his favor is as a cloud of the latter rain. [16] How much better is it to get wisdom than gold! Yea, to get understanding is rather to be chosen than silver. [17]The highway of the upright is to depart from evil: He that keepeth his way preserveth his soul. [18] Pride goeth before destruction, And a haughty spirit before a fall. [19]Better it is to be of a lowly spirit with the poor, Than to divide the spoil with the proud. [20] He that giveth heed unto the word shall find good; And whoso trusteth in Jehovah, happy is he. [21]The wise in heart shall be called prudent; And the sweetness of the lips increaseth learning. [22]Understanding is a well-spring of life unto him that hath it; But the correction of fools is their folly. [23] The heart of the wise instructeth his mouth, And addeth learning to his lips. [24] Pleasant words are as a honeycomb, Sweet to the soul, and health to the bones. [25]There is a way which seemeth right unto a man, But the end thereof are the ways of death. [26] The appetite of the laboring man laboreth for him; For his mouth urgeth him thereto. [27]A worthless man deviseth mischief; And in his lips there is as a scorching fire. [28] A perverse man scattereth abroad strife; And a whisperer separateth chief friends. [29]A man of violence enticeth his neighbor, And leadeth him in a way that is not good. [30] He that shutteth his eyes, it is to devise perverse things: He that compresseth his lips bringeth evil to pass. [31]The hoary head is a crown of glory; It shall be found in the way of righteousness. [32] He that is slow to anger is better than the mighty; And he that ruleth his spirit, than he that taketh a city. [33] The lot is cast into the lap; But the whole disposing thereof is of Jehovah.

Reading Plan:

☐ **Proverbs 17 – Friendship and Strife**

17 7 [1]Better is a dry morsel, and quietness therewith, Than a house full of feasting with strife. [2]A servant that dealeth wisely shall have rule over a son that causeth shame, And shall have part in the inheritance among the brethren. [3] The refining pot is for silver, and the furnace for gold; But Jehovah trieth the hearts. [4]An evil-doer giveth heed to wicked lips; And a liar giveth ear to a mischievous tongue. [5]Whoso mocketh the poor reproacheth his Maker; And he that is glad at calamity shall not be unpunished. [6] Children's children are the crown of old men; And the glory of children are their fathers. [7]Excellent speech becometh not a fool; Much less do lying lips a prince. [8] A bribe is as a precious stone in the eyes of him that hath it; Whithersoever it turneth, it prospereth. [9] He that covereth a transgression seeketh love; But he that harpeth on a matter separateth chief friends. [10] A rebuke entereth deeper into one that hath understanding Than a hundred stripes into a fool. [11]An evil man seeketh only rebellion; Therefore a cruel messenger shall be sent against him. [12] Let a bear robbed of her whelps meet a man, Rather than a fool in his folly. [13]Whoso rewardeth evil for good, Evil shall not depart from his house. [14] The beginning of strife is as when one letteth out water: Therefore leave off contention, before there is quarrelling. [15] He that justifieth the wicked, and he that condemneth the righteous, Both of them alike are an abomination to Jehovah. [16]Wherefore is there a price in the hand of a fool to buy wisdom, Seeing he hath no understanding? [17]A friend loveth at all times; And a brother is born for adversity. [18] A man void of understanding striketh hands, And becometh surety in the presence of his neighbor. ¹⁹ He loveth transgression that loveth strife: He that raiseth high his gate seeketh destruction. ²⁰ He that hath a wayward heart findeth no good; And he that hath a perverse tongue falleth into mischief. ²¹ He that begetteth a fool doeth it to his sorrow; And the father of a fool hath no joy. ²²A cheerful heart is a good medicine; But a broken spirit drieth up the bones. ²³A wicked man receiveth a bribe out of the bosom, To pervert the ways of justice. ²⁴Wisdom is before the face of him that hath understanding; But the eyes of a fool are in the ends of the earth. ²⁵A foolish son is a grief to his father, And bitterness to her that bare him. ²⁶Also to punish the righteous is not good, Nor to smite the noble for their uprightness. ²⁷ He that spareth his words hath knowledge; And he that is of a cool spirit is a man of understanding. ²⁸ Even a fool, when he holdeth his peace, is counted wise; When he shutteth his lips, he is esteemed as prudent.

Reading Plan:

☐ Proverbs 18 – The Power of Words

18 ¹ He that separateth himself seeketh his own desire, And rageth against all sound wisdom. ²A fool hath no delight in understanding, But only that his heart may reveal itself. ³When the wicked cometh, there cometh also contempt, And with ignominy cometh reproach. ⁴ The words of a man's mouth are as deep waters; The wellspring of wisdom is as a flowing brook. ⁵To respect the person of the wicked is not good, Nor to turn aside the righteous in judgment. ⁶A fool's lips enter into contention, And his mouth calleth for stripes. ⁷A fool's mouth is his destruction, And his lips are the snare of his soul. ⁸ The words of a whisperer are as dainty morsels, And they go down into the innermost parts. ⁹ He also that is slack in his work Is brother to him that is a destroyer. ¹⁰ The name of Jehovah is a strong tower; The righteous runneth into it, and is safe. ¹¹The rich man's wealth is his strong

city, And as a high wall in his own imagination. [12]Before destruction the heart of man is haughty; And before honor goeth humility. [13] He that giveth answer before he heareth, It is folly and shame unto him. [14] The spirit of a man will sustain his infirmity; But a broken spirit who can bear? [15]The heart of the prudent getteth knowledge; And the ear of the wise seeketh knowledge. [16]A man's gift maketh room for him, And bringeth him before great men. [17] He that pleadeth his cause first seemeth just; But his neighbor cometh and searcheth him out. [18] The lot causeth contentions to cease, And parteth between the mighty. [19]A brother offended is harder to be won than a strong city; And such contentions are like the bars of a castle. [20] A man's belly shall be filled with the fruit of his mouth; With the increase of his lips shall he be satisfied. [21]Death and life are in the power of the tongue; And they that love it shall eat the fruit thereof. [22]Whoso findeth a wife findeth a good thing, And obtaineth favor of Jehovah. [23] The poor useth entreaties; But the rich answereth roughly. [24] He that maketh many friends doeth it to his own destruction; But there is a friend that sticketh closer than a brother.

Reading Plan:

☐ **Proverbs 19 – Wisdom and Integrity**

19
[1]Better is the poor that walketh in his integrity Than he that is perverse in his lips and is a fool. [2]Also, that the soul be without knowledge is not good; And he that hasteth with his feet sinneth. [3] The foolishness of man subverteth his way; And his heart fretteth against Jehovah. [4]Wealth addeth many friends; But the poor is separated from his friend. [5]A false witness shall not be unpunished; And he that uttereth lies shall not escape. [6]Many will entreat the favor of the liberal man; And every man is a friend to him that giveth gifts. [7]All the brethren of the poor do hate him: How much more do his friends go far from him! He pursueth them with words, but they are gone. [8] He that getteth wisdom loveth his own soul: He that keepeth understanding shall find good. [9]A false witness shall not be unpunished; And he that uttereth

lies shall perish. [10]Delicate living is not seemly for a fool; Much less for a servant to have rule over princes. [11]The discretion of a man maketh him slow to anger; And it is his glory to pass over a transgression. [12] The king's wrath is as the roaring of a lion; But his favor is as dew upon the grass. [13]A foolish son is the calamity of his father; And the contentions of a wife are a continual dropping. [14] House and riches are an inheritance from fathers; But a prudent wife is from Jehovah. [15] Slothfulness casteth into a deep sleep; And the idle soul shall suffer hunger. [16] He that keepeth the commandment keepeth his soul; But he that is careless of his ways shall die. [17] He that hath pity upon the poor lendeth unto Jehovah, And his good deed will he pay him again. [18] Chasten thy son, seeing there is hope; And set not thy heart on his destruction. [19]A man of great wrath shall bear the penalty; For if thou deliver him, thou must do it yet again. [20] Hear counsel, and receive instruction, That thou mayest be wise in thy latter end. [21]There are many devices in a man's heart; But the counsel of Jehovah, that shall stand. [22] That which maketh a man to be desired is his kindness; And a poor man is better than a liar. [23] The fear of Jehovah tendeth to life; And he that hath it shall abide satisfied; He shall not be visited with evil. [24] The sluggard burieth his hand in the dish, And will not so much as bring it to his mouth again. [25] Smite a scoffer, and the simple will learn prudence; And reprove one that hath understanding, and he will understand knowledge. [26] He that doeth violence to his father, and chaseth away his mother, Is a son that causeth shame and bringeth reproach. [27]Cease, my son, to hear instruction Only to err from the words of knowledge. [28] A worthless witness mocketh at justice; And the mouth of the wicked swalloweth iniquity. [29] Judgments are prepared for scoffers, And stripes for the back of fools.

Teaching & Commentary

Proverbs 15 – Gentle Answers and Wise Words

It is amazing how much power we have in our words. With that comes responsibility. "A gentle answer turns away wrath, but harsh words stir up anger. "We are a snap-back culture, responding in haste to anything and everything, even the smallest thing we don't like. We like to argue. God wants us to be a peacemaking people. Disagreements are allowed, if we treat each other with dignity and respect. It builds trust and opens doors.

Proverbs 16 – Commit Your Plans to the Lord

In this chapter, Solomon shows that even the most carefully laid plans are directed by God. We can be wise when we are prudent and deliberate, but wiser still to commit our plans to God's direction. He also points out that pride goes before destruction, but a humble spirit goes before honor.

Proverbs 17 – Friendship and Strife

There are many proverbial jewels in this chapter on relationships. "A friend loves at all times." "To kindle strife is like breaking a dam." It illustrates how quickly a conflict can spin out of control, and why it is important to be loyal, forgiving, and slow to quarrel.

Proverbs 18 – The Power of Words

"The tongue has the power of life and death."

We've all seen, heard and experienced the results of words that can either cut or heal, build up or tear down. Words matter and the world around us is swimming with texts, posts, shares, likes, tweets, etc.... which is why it's never been more important to live out God's truth.

Proverbs 19 – Wisdom and Patience

This chapter is all about reminding us to be patient, bear with, slow to anger. It warns us against judging others or being wise in our own eyes. Wisdom is seeing the bigger picture and responding in a way that will honor God.

Bottom Line:

Your words and your attitude have a bigger impact on your relationships than you may think. Honor God by speaking gently, staying humble and loving in every situation, and you will build meaningful, long-lasting relationships that glorify Him.

Let's Talk About It

1. Which verse about words or speech stood out to you most this week?_

2. How can you practice gentleness and humility in your conversations?

3. Where have you seen pride damage a relationship?

4. What does it look like to commit your plans to the Lord in your relationships?

Apply It to Your Life

- **Day 1:** Think about a relationship that needs more gentleness or patience.

- **Day 2:** Pray for humility and wisdom in how you speak to others.

- **Day 3:** Choose one way to build someone up with your words today.

- **Day 4:** Reflect on any conflicts and ask God for help to bring peace.

Think About It & Do It

- **Speech Check:** Before speaking, ask, *"Will this bring life or harm?*
- **Verse Meditation:** Spend 5 minutes repeating Proverbs 15:1.
- **Relationship Journal:** Write about one friendship you're grateful for and how you can nurture it.

Memory Verse

"Better a little with the fear of the LORD than great wealth with turmoil."
- Proverbs 15:16

📙 It's time to Journal!

Reflect on how this week's teaching speaks to your current season of life. Now write it down.

Let's Pray

Lord, thank You for showing me how my words and actions matter. Help me to build others up with kindness and humility. Teach me to honor You in every relationship.

In Jesus' name, Amen.

Week 6- Words, Work and Wealth

Theme: Wise Living in Daily Life
Weekly Focus: Proverbs 20–24

Let's Pray

Father God, thank You for Your Word that teaches me how to live wisely. Help me honor You in my work, my words, and my daily choices. Show me how to build a life that reflects Your wisdom.

In Jesus' name, Amen.

Reading Plan:

☐ **Proverbs 20 – Integrity and Justice**

20 ¹Wine is a mocker, strong drink a brawler; And whosoever erreth thereby is not wise. ² The terror of a king is as the roaring of a lion: He that provoketh him to anger sinneth against his own life. ³ It is an honor for a man to keep aloof from strife; But every fool will be quarrelling. ⁴ The sluggard will not plow by reason of the winter; Therefore he shall beg in harvest, and have nothing. ⁵Counsel in the heart of man is like deep water; But a man of understanding will draw it out. ⁶Most men will proclaim every one his own kindness; But a faithful man who can find? ⁷A righteous man that walketh in his integrity, Blessed are his children after him. ⁸ A king that sitteth on the throne of judgment Scattereth away all evil with his eyes. ⁹Who can say, I have made my heart clean, I am pure from my sin? ¹⁰Diverse weights, and diverse measures, Both of them alike are an abomination to Jehovah. ¹¹Even a child maketh himself known by his doings, Whether his work be pure, and whether it be right. ¹² The hearing ear, and the seeing eye, Jehovah hath made even both of them. ¹³ Love not sleep, lest thou come to poverty; Open thine eyes, and thou shalt be satisfied with bread. ¹⁴ It is bad, it is bad, saith the buyer; But when he is gone his way, then he boasteth. ¹⁵There is gold, and abundance of rubies;

But the lips of knowledge are a precious jewel. [16] Take his garment that is surety for a stranger; And hold him in pledge that is surety for foreigners. [17]Bread of falsehood is sweet to a man; But afterwards his mouth shall be filled with gravel. [18] Every purpose is established by counsel; And by wise guidance make thou war. [19] He that goeth about as a tale-bearer revealeth secrets; Therefore company not with him that openeth wide his lips. [20]Whoso curseth his father or his mother, His lamp shall be put out in blackness of darkness. [21]An inheritance may be gotten hastily at the beginning; But the end thereof shall not be blessed. [22] Say not thou, I will recompense evil: Wait for Jehovah, and he will save thee. [23]Diverse weights are an abomination to Jehovah; And a false balance is not good. [24]A man's goings are of Jehovah; How then can man understand his way? [25] It is a snare to a man rashly to say, It is holy, And after vows to make inquiry. [26]A wise king winnoweth the wicked, And bringeth the threshing-wheel over them. [27]The spirit of man is the lamp of Jehovah, Searching all his innermost parts. [28]Kindness and truth preserve the king; And his throne is upholden by kindness. [29] The glory of young men is their strength; And the beauty of old men is the hoary head. [30] Stripes that wound cleanse away evil; And strokes reach the innermost parts.

Reading Plan:

☐ **Proverbs 21 – Righteousness and Humility**

21

[1]The king's heart is in the hand of Jehovah as the watercourses: He turneth it whithersoever he will. [2]Every way of a man is right in his own eyes; But Jehovah weigheth the hearts. [3] To do righteousness and justice Is more acceptable to Jehovah than sacrifice. [4]A high look, and a proud heart, Even the lamp of the wicked, is sin. [5]The thoughts of the diligent tend only to plenteousness; But every one that is hasty hasteth only to want. [6] The getting of treasures by a lying tongue Is a vapor driven to and fro by them that seek death. [7]The violence of the wicked shall sweep them away, Because they refuse to do justice. [8] The way of him that is laden with

guilt is exceeding crooked; But as for the pure, his work is right. [9] It is better to dwell in the corner of the housetop, Than with a contentious woman in a wide house. [10] The soul of the wicked desireth evil: His neighbor findeth no favor in his eyes. [11]When the scoffer is punished, the simple is made wise; And when the wise is instructed, he receiveth knowledge. [12] The righteous man considereth the house of the wicked, How the wicked are overthrown to their ruin. [13]Whoso stoppeth his ears at the cry of the poor, He also shall cry, but shall not be heard. [14]A gift in secret pacifieth anger; And a present in the bosom, strong wrath. [15] It is joy to the righteous to do justice; But it is a destruction to the workers of iniquity. [16] The man that wandereth out of the way of understanding Shall rest in the assembly of the dead. [17] He that loveth pleasure shall be a poor man: He that loveth wine and oil shall not be rich. [18] The wicked is a ransom for the righteous; And the treacherous cometh in the stead of the upright. [19] It is better to dwell in a desert land, Than with a contentious and fretful woman. [20] There is precious treasure and oil in the dwelling of the wise; But a foolish man swalloweth it up. [21] He that followeth after righteousness and kindness Findeth life, righteousness, and honor. [22]A wise man scaleth the city of the mighty, And bringeth down the strength of the confidence thereof. [23]Whoso keepeth his mouth and his tongue Keepeth his soul from troubles. [24] The proud and haughty man, scoffer is his name; He worketh in the arrogance of pride. [25]The desire of the sluggard killeth him; For his hands refuse to labor. [26] There is that coveteth greedily all the day long; But the righteous giveth and withholdeth not. [27]The sacrifice of the wicked is an abomination; How much more, when he bringeth it with a wicked mind! [28] A false witness shall perish; But the man that heareth shall speak so as to endure. [29]A wicked man hardeneth his face; But as for the upright, he establisheth his ways. [30] There is no wisdom nor understanding Nor counsel against Jehovah. [31]The horse is prepared against the day of battle; But victory is of Jehovah.

Reading Plan:

☐ Proverbs 22 – A Good Name and Generosity

22 ¹A good name is rather to be chosen than great riches, And loving favor rather than silver and gold. ² The rich and the poor meet together: Jehovah is the maker of them all. ³A prudent man seeth the evil, and hideth himself; But the simple pass on, and suffer for it. ⁴ The reward of humility and the fear of Jehovah Is riches, and honor, and life. ⁵Thorns and snares are in the way of the perverse: He that keepeth his soul shall be far from them. ⁶ Train up a child in the way he should go, And even when he is old he will not depart from it. ⁷The rich ruleth over the poor; And the borrower is servant to the lender. ⁸ He that soweth iniquity shall reap calamity; And the rod of his wrath shall fail. ⁹ He that hath a bountiful eye shall be blessed; For he giveth of his bread to the poor. ¹⁰ Cast out the scoffer, and contention will go out; Yea, strife and ignominy will cease. ¹¹ He that loveth pureness of heart, For the grace of his lips the king will be his friend. ¹² The eyes of Jehovah preserve him that hath knowledge; But he overthroweth the words of the treacherous man. ¹³ The sluggard saith, There is a lion without; I shall be slain in the streets. ¹⁴ The mouth of strange women is a deep pit; He that is abhorred of Jehovah shall fall therein. ¹⁵ Foolishness is bound up in the heart of a child; But the rod of correction shall drive it far from him. ¹⁶ He that oppresseth the poor to increase his gain, And he that giveth to the rich, shall come only to want. ¹⁷ Incline thine ear, and hear the words of the wise, And apply thy heart unto my knowledge. ¹⁸ For it is a pleasant thing if thou keep them within thee, If they be established together upon thy lips. ¹⁹ That thy trust may be in Jehovah, I have made them known to thee this day, even to thee. ²⁰ Have not I written unto thee excellent things Of counsels and knowledge, ²¹To make thee know the certainty of the words of truth, That thou mayest carry back words of truth to them that send thee? ²² Rob not the poor, because he is poor; Neither oppress the afflicted in the gate: ²³ For Jehovah will plead their cause, And despoil of life those that despoil them. ²⁴Make no friendship with a man that is given to anger; And with a wrathful man

thou shalt not go: [25]Lest thou learn his ways, And get a snare to thy soul.
[26]Be thou not one of them that strike hands, Or of them that are sureties
for debts. [27] If thou hast not wherewith to pay, Why should he take away
thy bed from under thee? [28] Remove not the ancient landmark, Which
thy fathers have set. [29] Seest thou a man diligent in his business? he shall
stand before kings; He shall not stand before mean men.

Reading Plan:

☐ Proverbs 23 – Warnings About Overindulgence

23 [1]When thou sittest to eat with a ruler, Consider diligently
him that is before thee; [2]And put a knife to thy throat, If
thou be a man given to appetite. [3]Be not desirous of his
dainties; Seeing they are deceitful food. [4]Weary not thyself to be rich;
Cease from thine own wisdom. [5]Wilt thou set thine eyes upon that which
is not? For riches certainly make themselves wings, Like an eagle that
flieth toward heaven. [6]Eat thou not the bread of him that hath an evil
eye, Neither desire thou his dainties: [7]For as he thinketh within himself,
so is he: Eat and drink, saith he to thee; But his heart is not with thee. [8]
The morsel which thou hast eaten shalt thou vomit up, And lose thy
sweet words. [9] Speak not in the hearing of a fool; For he will despise the
wisdom of thy words. [10]Remove not the ancient landmark; And enter not
into the fields of the fatherless: [11]For their Redeemer is strong; He will
plead their cause against thee. [12]Apply thy heart unto instruction, And
thine ears to the words of knowledge. [13]Withhold not correction from
the child; For if thou beat him with the rod, he will not die. [14] Thou shalt
beat him with the rod, And shalt deliver his soul from Sheol. [15]My son, if
thy heart be wise, My heart will be glad, even mine: [16] Yea, my heart will
rejoice, When thy lips speak right things. [17]Let not thy heart envy sinners;
But be thou in the fear of Jehovah all the day long: [18] For surely there is a
reward; And thy hope shall not be cut off. [19] Hear thou, my son, and be
wise, And guide thy heart in the way. [20] Be not among winebibbers,
Among gluttonous eaters of flesh: [21]For the drunkard and the glutton

shall come to poverty; And drowsiness will clothe a man with rags. [22] Hearken unto thy father that begat thee, And despise not thy mother when she is old. [23]Buy the truth, and sell it not; Yea, wisdom, and instruction, and understanding. [24] The father of the righteous will greatly rejoice; And he that begetteth a wise child will have joy of him. [25]Let thy father and thy mother be glad, And let her that bare thee rejoice. [26]My son, give me thy heart; And let thine eyes delight in my ways. [27]For a harlot is a deep ditch; And a foreign woman is a narrow pit. [28] Yea, she lieth in wait as a robber, And increaseth the treacherous among men. [29]Who hath woe? who hath sorrow? who hath contentions? Who hath complaining? who hath wounds without cause? Who hath redness of eyes? [30] They that tarry long at the wine; They that go to seek out mixed wine. [31]Look not thou upon the wine when it is red, When it sparkleth in the cup, When it goeth down smoothly: [32]At the last it biteth like a serpent, And stingeth like an adder. [33] Thine eyes shall behold strange things, And thy heart shall utter perverse things. [34] Yea, thou shalt be as he that lieth down in the midst of the sea, Or as he that lieth upon the top of a mast. [35]They have stricken me, shalt thou say, and I was not hurt; They have beaten me, and I felt it not: When shall I awake? I will seek it yet again.

Reading Plan:

☐ **Proverbs 24 – Wisdom in Action**

2 4 [1]Be not thou envious against evil men; Neither desire to be with them: [2] For their heart studieth oppression, And their lips talk of mischief. [3] Through wisdom is a house builded; And by understanding it is established; [4]And by knowledge are the chambers filled With all precious and pleasant riches. [5]A wise man is strong; Yea, a man of knowledge increaseth might. [6] For by wise guidance thou shalt make thy war; And in the multitude of counsellors there is safety. [7]Wisdom is too high for a fool: He openeth not his mouth in the gate. [8] He that deviseth to do evil, Men shall call him a mischief-maker. [9]

The thought of foolishness is sin; And the scoffer is an abomination to men. [10] If thou faint in the day of adversity, Thy strength is small. [11]Deliver them that are carried away unto death, And those that are ready to be slain see that thou hold back. [12] If thou sayest, Behold, we knew not this; Doth not he that weigheth the hearts consider it? And he that keepeth thy soul, doth not he know it? And shall not he render to every man according to his work? [13]My son, eat thou honey, for it is good; And the droppings of the honeycomb, which are sweet to thy taste: [14] So shalt thou know wisdom to be unto thy soul; If thou hast found it, then shall there be a reward, And thy hope shall not be cut off. [15]Lay not wait, O wicked man, against the habitation of the righteous; Destroy not his resting-place: [16] For a righteous man falleth seven times, and riseth up again; But the wicked are overthrown by calamity. [17]Rejoice not when thine enemy falleth, And let not thy heart be glad when he is overthrown; [18] Lest Jehovah see it, and it displease him, And he turn away his wrath from him. [19] Fret not thyself because of evil-doers; Neither be thou envious at the wicked: [20] For there shall be no reward to the evil man; The lamp of the wicked shall be put out. [21]My son, fear thou Jehovah and the king; And company not with them that are given to change: [22] For their calamity shall rise suddenly; And the destruction from them both, who knoweth it? [23] These also are sayings of the wise. To have respect of persons in judgment is not good. [24] He that saith unto the wicked, Thou art righteous, Peoples shall curse him, nations shall abhor him; [25]But to them that rebuke him shall be delight, And a good blessing shall come upon them. [26] He kisseth the lips Who giveth a right answer. [27]Prepare thy work without, And make it ready for thee in the field; And afterwards build thy house. [28] Be not a witness against thy neighbor without cause; And deceive not with thy lips. [29] Say not, I will do so to him as he hath done to me; I will render to the man according to his work. [30] I went by the field of the sluggard, And by the vineyard of the man void of understanding; [31]And, lo, it was all grown over with thorns, The face thereof was covered with nettles, And the stone wall thereof was broken down. [32] Then I beheld, and considered well; I saw, and received instruction: [33] Yet a little sleep, a little slumber, A little folding of the hands to sleep; [34] So shall thy poverty come as a robber, And thy want as an armed man.

Teaching & Commentary

Proverbs 20 – Integrity and Justice

This chapter emphasizes honesty and fairness. It warns against dishonesty in business and says that the Lord detests double standards. In today's world, this might look like being truthful at work, keeping your commitments, and treating others with respect even when no one is watching.

Proverbs 21 – Righteousness and Humility

"Doing what is right and just is more acceptable to the LORD than sacrifice."

Proverbs 21:3 NLT

Again, Solomon teaches that God cares about our lives, our righteous, humble living, and less about empty religious rituals.

Proverbs 22 – A Good Name and Generosity

"The name of the LORD is a strong tower; the righteous run to it and are safe. "

- Proverbs 22:27 NLT

This chapter is all about good reputation through being generous. It illustrates how a "good name" means much more than money, and that we should not exploit the poor or oppress one another.

Proverbs 23 – Warnings About Overindulgence

"Do not wear yourself out to get rich; do not trust your own cleverness."
- Proverbs 23:4 NLT

Here, Solomon is warning against the pursuit of wealth at any costs; he's also cautioning against over-indulgence in eating and drinking, because this will cause a person to fall.

Proverbs 24 – Wisdom in Action

"When you see the oppression of the poor and the taking of unjust judgment, do not be surprised."

- Proverbs 24:15 NLT

In this chapter, Solomon is calling us to be strong in the day of trouble, and deliver the victim from the oppressor, while also warning us to shun evil.

Bottom Line:

Wisdom isn't just something you believe—it's something you live. It shapes your work, your reputation, your habits, and your compassion for others.

Let's Talk About It

1. Which verse stood out to you the most this week?

2. Where in your life is it hardest to practice self-control or contentment?

3. What does it look like to have a good name in your community?

4. How can you put wisdom into action this week?

Apply It to Your Life

- **Day 1:** Reflect on where you need to be more honest or fair.

- **Day 2:** Pray for self-control in an area where you feel tempted to overdo.

- **Day 3:** Think about how you can be more generous or compassionate.

- **Day 4:** Find a habit you want to change and ask God for help.

Think About It & Do It

- **Integrity Check:** Before making decisions, ask: *Is this honest?*

- **Verse Meditation:** Spend 5 minutes repeating Proverbs 16:3.

- **Wisdom Journal:** Write about one area where you practiced self-control.

Memory Verse

"The plans of the diligent lead to profit as surely as haste leads to poverty."

- Proverbs 21:5

📖 It's time to Journal!

Reflect on how this week's teaching speaks to your current season of life. Now write it down.

Let's Pray

Lord, thank You for showing me how to live wisely every day. Help me to be honest, generous, and self-controlled. Teach me to commit all my work and plans to You.

In Jesus' name, Amen.

Week 7: Humility and Leadership

Theme: Cultivating a Teachable Spirit
Weekly Focus: Proverbs 25–29

Let's Pray

Father God, thank You for placing people in my life who help me grow. Teach me to be humble and open to correction. Show me how to be a wise leader and a teachable follower.

In Jesus' name, Amen.

Reading Plan:

☐ **Proverbs 25 – More Proverbs of Solomon: Self-Control and Honor**

25 [1]These also are proverbs of Solomon, which the men of Hezekiah king of Judah copied out. [2] It is the glory of God to conceal a thing; But the glory of kings is to search out a matter. [3]As the heavens for height, and the earth for depth, So the heart of kings is unsearchable. [4] Take away the dross from the silver, And there cometh forth a vessel for the refiner: [5]Take away the wicked from before the king, And his throne shall be established in righteousness. [6] Put not thyself forward in the presence of the king, And stand not in the place of great men: [7]For better is it that it be said unto thee, Come up hither, Than that thou shouldest be put lower in the presence of the prince, Whom thine eyes have seen. [8]Go not forth hastily to strive, Lest thou know not what to do in the end thereof, When thy neighbor hath put thee to shame. [9]Debate thy cause with thy neighbor himself, And disclose not the secret of another; [10] Lest he that heareth it revile thee, And thine infamy turn not away. [11]A word fitly spoken Is like apples of gold in network of silver. [12]As an ear-ring of gold, and an ornament of fine gold, So is a wise reprover upon an obedient ear. [13]As the cold of snow in the time of harvest, So is a faithful messenger to them that send him; For he refresheth the soul of his masters. [14]As clouds and wind without rain, So

is he that boasteth himself of his gifts falsely. [15]By long forbearing is a ruler persuaded, And a soft tongue breaketh the bone. [16] Hast thou found honey? eat so much as is sufficient for thee, Lest thou be filled therewith, and vomit it. [17]Let thy foot be seldom in thy neighbor's house, Lest he be weary of thee, and hate thee. [18] A man that beareth false witness against his neighbor Is a maul, and a sword, and a sharp arrow. [19] Confidence in an unfaithful man in time of trouble Is like a broken tooth, and a foot out of joint. [20] As one that taketh off a garment in cold weather, and as vinegar upon soda, So is he that singeth songs to a heavy heart. [21] If thine enemy be hungry, give him bread to eat; And if he be thirsty, give him water to drink: [22] For thou wilt heap coals of fire upon his head, And Jehovah will reward thee. [23] The north wind bringeth forth rain; So doth a backbiting tongue an angry countenance. [24] It is better to dwell in the corner of the housetop, Than with a contentious woman in a wide house. [25]As cold waters to a thirsty soul, So is good news from a far country. [26]As a troubled fountain, and a corrupted spring, So is a righteous man that giveth way before the wicked. [27] It is not good to eat much honey; So for men to search out their own glory is grievous. [28] He whose spirit is without restraint Is like a city that is broken down and without walls.

Reading Plan:

☐ **Proverbs 26 – Fools and Sluggards**

26 [1]As snow in summer, and as rain in harvest, So honor is not seemly for a fool. [2]As the sparrow in her wandering, as the swallow in her flying, So the curse that is causeless alighteth not. [3]A whip for the horse, a bridle for the ass, And a rod for the back of fools. [4]Answer not a fool according to his folly, Lest thou also be like unto him. [5]Answer a fool according to his folly, Lest he be wise in his own conceit. [6] He that sendeth a message by the hand of a fool Cutteth off his own feet, and drinketh in damage. [7]The legs of the lame hang loose; So is a parable in the mouth of fools. [8] As one that bindeth a stone in a sling, So is he that giveth honor to a fool. ⁹As a thorn that goeth up into the hand of a drunkard, So is a parable in the mouth of fools. ¹⁰ As an archer that woundeth all, So is he that hireth a fool and he that hireth them that pass by. ¹¹As a dog that returneth to his vomit, So is a fool that repeateth his folly. ¹² Seest thou a man wise in his own conceit? There is more hope of a fool than of him. ¹³ The sluggard saith, There is a lion in the way; A lion is in the streets. ¹⁴As the door turneth upon its hinges, So doth the sluggard upon his bed. ¹⁵The sluggard burieth his hand in the dish; It wearieth him to bring it again to his mouth. ¹⁶ The sluggard is wiser in his own conceit Than seven men that can render a reason. ¹⁷ He that passeth by, and vexeth himself with strife belonging not to him, Is like one that taketh a dog by the ears. ¹⁸ As a madman who casteth firebrands, Arrows, and death, ¹⁹ So is the man that deceiveth his neighbor, And saith, Am not I in sport? ²⁰ For lack of wood the fire goeth out; And where there is no whisperer, contention ceaseth. ²¹As coals are to hot embers, and wood to fire, So is a contentious man to inflame strife. ²² The words of a whisperer are as dainty morsels, And they go down into the innermost parts. ²³ Fervent lips and a wicked heart Are like an earthen vessel overlaid with silver dross. ²⁴ He that hateth dissembleth with his lips; But he layeth up deceit within him: ²⁵When he speaketh fair, believe him not; For there are seven abominations in his heart: ²⁶ Though his hatred cover itself with guile, His wickedness shall be openly showed before the assembly. ²⁷Whoso diggeth a pit shall fall therein; And he that rolleth a stone, it shall return upon him. ²⁸ A lying tongue hateth those whom it hath wounded; And a flattering mouth worketh ruin.

Reading Plan:

☐ **Proverbs 27 – Friendship and Integrity**

27
¹Boast not thyself of to-morrow; For thou knowest not what a day may bring forth. ² Let another man praise thee, and not thine own mouth; A stranger, and not thine own lips. ³A stone is heavy, and the sand weighty; But a fool's vexation is

heavier than they both. ⁴Wrath is cruel, and anger is overwhelming; But who is able to stand before jealousy? ⁵Better is open rebuke Than love that is hidden. ⁶ Faithful are the wounds of a friend; But the kisses of an enemy are profuse. ⁷The full soul loatheth a honeycomb; But to the hungry soul every bitter thing is sweet. ⁸ As a bird that wandereth from her nest, So is a man that wandereth from his place. ⁹Oil and perfume rejoice the heart; So doth the sweetness of a man's friend that cometh of hearty counsel. ¹⁰ Thine own friend, and thy father's friend, forsake not; And go not to thy brother's house in the day of thy calamity: Better is a neighbor that is near than a brother far off. ¹¹My son, be wise, and make my heart glad, That I may answer him that reproacheth me. ¹²A prudent man seeth the evil, and hideth himself; But the simple pass on, and suffer for it. ¹³ Take his garment that is surety for a stranger; And hold him in pledge that is surety for a foreign woman. ¹⁴ He that blesseth his friend with a loud voice, rising early in the morning, It shall be counted a curse to him. ¹⁵A continual dropping in a very rainy day And a contentious woman are alike: ¹⁶ He that would restrain her restraineth the wind; And his right hand encountereth oil. ¹⁷ Iron sharpeneth iron; So a man sharpeneth the countenance of his friend. ¹⁸Whoso keepeth the fig-tree shall eat the fruit thereof; And he that regardeth his master shall be honored. ¹⁹As in water face answereth to face, So the heart of man to man. ²⁰ Sheol and Abaddon are never satisfied; And the eyes of man are never satisfied. ²¹The refining pot is for silver, and the furnace for gold; And a man is tried by his praise. ²² Though thou shouldest bray a fool in a mortar with a pestle along with bruised grain, Yet will not his foolishness depart from him. ²³Be thou diligent to know the state of thy flocks, And look well to thy herds: ²⁴ For riches are not for ever; And doth the crown endure unto all generations? ²⁵The hay is carried, and the tender grass showeth itself, And the herbs of the mountains are gathered in. ²⁶ The lambs are for thy clothing, And the goats are the price of the field; ²⁷And there will be goats' milk enough for thy food, for the food of thy household, And maintenance for thy maidens.

Reading Plan:

☐ **Proverbs 28 – Boldness and Integrity**

28

[1]The wicked flee when no man pursueth; But the righteous are bold as a lion. [2]For the transgression of a land many are the princes thereof; But by men of understanding and knowledge the state thereof shall be prolonged. [3]A needy man that oppresseth the poor Is like a sweeping rain which leaveth no food. [4]They that forsake the law praise the wicked; But such as keep the law contend with them. [5]Evil men understand not justice; But they that seek Jehovah understand all things. [6]Better is the poor that walketh in his integrity, Than he that is perverse in his ways, though he be rich. [7]Whoso keepeth the law is a wise son; But he that is a companion of gluttons shameth his father. [8] He that augmenteth his substance by interest and increase, Gathereth it for him that hath pity on the poor. [9] He that turneth away his ear from hearing the law, Even his prayer is an abomination. [10]Whoso causeth the upright to go astray in an evil way, He shall fall himself into his own pit; But the perfect shall inherit good. [11]The rich man is wise in his own conceit; But the poor that hath understanding searcheth him out. [12]When the righteous triumph, there is great glory; But when the wicked rise, men hide themselves. [13] He that covereth his transgressions shall not prosper; But whoso confesseth and forsaketh them shall obtain mercy. [14] Happy is the man that feareth alway; But he that hardeneth his heart shall fall into mischief. [15]As a roaring lion, and a ranging bear, So is a wicked ruler over a poor people. [16] The prince that lacketh understanding is also a great oppressor; But he that hateth covetousness shall prolong his days. [17]A man that is laden with the blood of any person Shall flee unto the pit; let no man stay him. [18]Whoso walketh uprightly shall be delivered; But he that is perverse in his ways shall fall at once. [19] He that tilleth his land shall have plenty of bread; But he that followeth after vain persons shall have poverty enough. [20] A faithful man shall abound with blessings; But he that maketh haste to be rich shall not be unpunished. [21]To have respect of persons is not good; Neither that a man should transgress for a piece of bread. [22] He that hath an evil eye hasteth after

riches, And knoweth not that want shall come upon him. ²³ He that rebuketh a man shall afterward find more favor Than he that flattereth with the tongue. ²⁴Whoso robbeth his father or his mother, and saith, It is no transgression, The same is the companion of a destroyer. ²⁵ He that is of a greedy spirit stirreth up strife; But he that putteth his trust in Jehovah shall be made fat. ²⁶ He that trusteth in his own heart is a fool; But whoso walketh wisely, he shall be delivered. ²⁷ He that giveth unto the poor shall not lack; But he that hideth his eyes shall have many a curse. ²⁸When the wicked rise, men hide themselves; But when they perish, the righteous increase.

Reading Plan:

☐ **Proverbs 29 – Righteous Leadership**

29 ¹ He that being often reproved hardeneth his neck Shall suddenly be destroyed, and that without remedy. ²When the righteous are increased, the people rejoice; But when a wicked man beareth rule, the people sigh. ³Whoso loveth wisdom rejoiceth his father; But he that keepeth company with harlots wasteth his substance. ⁴ The king by justice establisheth the land; But he that exacteth gifts overthroweth it. ⁵A man that flattereth his neighbor Spreadeth a net for his steps. ⁶ In the transgression of an evil man there is a snare; But the righteous doth sing and rejoice. ⁷The righteous taketh knowledge of the cause of the poor; The wicked hath not understanding to know it. ⁸ Scoffers set a city in a flame; But wise men turn away wrath. ⁹ If a wise man hath a controversy with a foolish man, Whether he be angry or laugh, there will be no rest. ¹⁰ The bloodthirsty hate him that is perfect; And as for the upright, they seek his life. ¹¹A fool uttereth all his anger; But a wise man keepeth it back and stilleth it. ¹² If a ruler hearkeneth to falsehood, All his servants are wicked. ¹³ The poor man and the oppressor meet together; Jehovah lighteneth the eyes of them both. ¹⁴ The king that faithfully judgeth the poor, His throne shall be established for ever. ¹⁵The rod and reproof give wisdom; But a child left to himself causeth shame to his mother. [16]When the wicked are increased, transgression increaseth; But the righteous shall look upon their fall. [17]Correct thy son, and he will give thee rest; Yea, he will give delight unto thy soul. [18]Where there is no vision, the people cast off restraint; But he that keepeth the law, happy is he. [19]A servant will not be corrected by words; For though he understand, he will not give heed. [20] Seest thou a man that is hasty in his words? There is more hope of a fool than of him. [21] He that delicately bringeth up his servant from a child Shall have him become a son at the last. [22]An angry man stirreth up strife, And a wrathful man aboundeth in transgression. [23]A man's pride shall bring him low; But he that is of a lowly spirit shall obtain honor. [24]Whoso is partner with a thief hateth his own soul; He heareth the adjuration and uttereth nothing. [25]The fear of man bringeth a snare; But whoso putteth his trust in Jehovah shall be safe. [26]Many seek the ruler's favor; But a man's judgment cometh from Jehovah. [27]An unjust man is an abomination to the righteous; And he that is upright in the way is an abomination to the wicked

Teaching & Commentary

Proverbs 25 – Self-Control and Honor

This chapter is about the importance of being in control of your words and emotions. Proverbs 25 emphasize that when we are patient and deliberate, we earn respect from others. In a world where, in a conversation, everyone is reacting quickly and publicly, the advice in Proverbs 25 reminds us to stop and respond from a place of wisdom.

Proverbs 26 – Fools and Sluggards

Solomon does an excellent job illustrating laziness and foolishness. He says that the lazy man is like a door on its hinges (it moves but goes nowhere). These verses serve as great reminders to take responsibility for ourselves, and avoid being stuck in self-destructive patterns.

Proverbs 27 – Friendship and Integrity

This chapter was cool in highlighting having honest friends. "Wounds from a friend can be trusted". Faithful friends tell us the truth in love even when we may not always want to hear it. This is also where we read about how "iron sharpens iron." God uses relationships to shape us.

Proverbs 28 – Boldness and Integrity

Here we see the righteous are as bold as a lion. Integrity provides confidence because you have nothing to hide. This chapter also warns that the concealer of sin will not prosper but whoever confesses and turns from their sins will be shown mercy.

Proverbs 29 – Righteous Leadership

Solomon illustrates how leadership affects everyone below them; when righteous leadership is present, the people in turn prosper. Even if you're not in a formal leadership role, you influence others by the example you set.

Bottom Line:

Wisdom means staying humble, being willing to learn, and surrounding yourself with people who sharpen your character. True leadership begins with integrity and a teachable spirit.

Let's Talk About It

1. What does it look like to be "iron sharpening iron" in your relationships?

2. Where do you struggle most with self-control or laziness?

3. How does humility help you grow in wisdom?

4. What's one area where you could lead by example this week?

Apply It to Your Life

- **Day 1:** Reflect on how you respond to correction—do you get defensive or listen?

- **Day 2:** Thank a friend who has spoken truth into your life.

- **Day 3:** Choose one area where you want to practice self-control.

- **Day 4:** Pray for God to show you how to lead others with integrity.

Think About It & Do It

- **Feedback Reflection:** Think about a time someone corrected you. What did you learn?

- **Verse Meditation:** Spend 5 minutes repeating Proverbs 27:17.

- **Wisdom Journal:** Write about one lesson you've learned from a friend or mentor.

Memory Verse

"As iron sharpens iron, so one person sharpens another."
- Proverbs 27:17

📖 It's time to Journal!

Reflect on how this week's teaching speaks to your current season of life. Now write it down.

Let's Pray

Lord, thank You for the people You've placed in my life to help me grow. Teach me to be humble and open to learning. Show me how to lead with integrity and to sharpen others as they sharpen me.

In Jesus' name, Amen.

Week 8: Virtue and Vision

Theme: Finishing Well
Weekly Focus: Proverbs 30–31

Let's Pray

Father God, thank You for the wisdom in these chapters. Teach me to value what matters most—character, humility, and reverence for You. Help me finish this study with a heart committed to living wisely.

In Jesus' name, Amen.

Reading Plan:

☐ **Proverbs 30 – The Sayings of Agur: Humility and Wonder**

30

[1]The words of Agur the son of Jakeh; the oracle. The man saith unto Ithiel, unto Ithiel and Ucal: [2] Surely I am more brutish than any man, And have not the understanding of a man; [3]And I have not learned wisdom, Neither have I the knowledge of the Holy One. [4]Who hath ascended up into heaven, and descended? Who hath gathered the wind in his fists? Who hath bound the waters in his garment? Who hath established all the ends of the earth? What is his name, and what is his son's name, if thou knowest? [5]Every word of God is tried: He is a shield unto them that take refuge in him. [6]Add thou not unto his words, Lest he reprove thee, and thou be found a liar. [7]Two things have I asked of thee; Deny me them not before I die: [8]Remove far from me falsehood and lies; Give me neither poverty nor riches; Feed me with the food that is needful for me: [9] Lest I be full, and deny thee, and say, Who is Jehovah? Or lest I be poor, and steal, And use profanely the name of my God. [10] Slander not a servant unto his master, Lest he curse thee, and thou be held guilty. [11]There is a generation that curse their father, And bless not their mother. [12] There is a generation that are pure in their own eyes, And yet are not washed from their filthiness. [13] There is a generation, oh how lofty are their eyes! And their eyelids are lifted up.

[14] There is a generation whose teeth are as swords, and their jaw teeth as knives, To devour the poor from off the earth, and the needy from among men. [15]The horseleach hath two daughters, crying, Give, give. There are three things that are never satisfied, Yea, four that say not, Enough: [16] Sheol; and the barren womb; The earth that is not satisfied with water; And the fire that saith not, Enough. [17]The eye that mocketh at his father, And despiseth to obey his mother, The ravens of the valley shall pick it out, And the young eagles shall eat it. [18] There are three things which are too wonderful for me, Yea, four which I know not: [19] The way of an eagle in the air; The way of a serpent upon a rock; The way of a ship in the midst of the sea; And the way of a man with a maiden. [20] So is the way of an adulterous woman; She eateth, and wipeth her mouth, And saith, I have done no wickedness. [21]For three things the earth doth tremble, And for four, which it cannot bear: [22] For a servant when he is king; And a fool when he is filled with food; [23] For an odious woman when she is married; And a handmaid that is heir to her mistress. [24] There are four things which are little upon the earth, But they are exceeding wise: [25]The ants are a people not strong, Yet they provide their food in the summer; [26] The conies are but a feeble folk, Yet make they their houses in the rocks; [27]The locusts have no king, Yet go they forth all of them by bands; [28] The lizard taketh hold with her hands, Yet is she in kings' palaces. [29] There are three things which are stately in their march, Yea, four which are stately in going: [30] The lion, which is mightiest among beasts, And turneth not away for any; [31]The greyhound; the he-goat also; And the king against whom there is no rising up. [32] If thou hast done foolishly in lifting up thyself, Or if thou hast thought evil, Lay thy hand upon thy mouth. [33] For the churning of milk bringeth forth butter, And the wringing of the nose bringeth forth blood; So the forcing of wrath bringeth forth strife.

Reading Plan:

☐ **Proverbs 31 – The Sayings of King Lemuel & The Virtuous Woman**

31

[1]The words of king Lemuel; the oracle which his mother taught him. [2]What, my son? and what, O son of my womb? And what, O son of my vows? [3]Give not thy strength unto women, Nor thy ways to that which destroyeth kings. [4]It is not for kings, O Lemuel, it is not for kings to drink wine; Nor for princes to say, Where is strong drink? [5]Lest they drink, and forget the law, And pervert the justice due to any that is afflicted. [6]Give strong drink unto him that is ready to perish, And wine unto the bitter in soul: [7]Let him drink, and forget his poverty, And remember his misery no more. [8]Open thy mouth for the dumb, In the cause of all such as are left desolate. [9]Open thy mouth, judge righteously, And minister justice to the poor and needy. [10] A worthy woman who can find? For her price is far above rubies. [11]The heart of her husband trusteth in her, And he shall have no lack of gain. [12] She doeth him good and not evil All the days of her life. [13] She seeketh wool and flax, And worketh willingly with her hands. [14] She is like the merchant-ships; She bringeth her bread from afar. [15] She riseth also while it is yet night, And giveth food to her household, And their task to her maidens. [16] She considereth a field, and buyeth it; With the fruit of her hands she planteth a vineyard. [17]She girdeth her loins with strength, And maketh strong her arms. [18] She perceiveth that her merchandise is profitable; Her lamp goeth not out by night. [19] She layeth her hands to the distaff, And her hands hold the spindle. [20] She stretcheth out her hand to the poor; Yea, she reacheth forth her hands to the needy. [21]She is not afraid of the snow for her household; For all her household are clothed with scarlet. [22] She maketh for herself carpets of tapestry; Her clothing is fine linen and purple. [23] Her husband is known in the gates, When he sitteth among the elders of the land. [24] She maketh linen garments and selleth them, And delivereth girdles unto the merchant. [25] Strength and dignity are her clothing; And she laugheth at the time to come. [26] She openeth her mouth with wisdom; And the law of kindness is on her tongue. [27] She looketh well to the ways of her household, And eateth not the bread of idleness. [28] Her children rise up, and call her blessed; Her husband also, and he praiseth her, saying: [29]Many daughters have done worthily, But thou excellest them all. [30]Grace is deceitful, and

beauty is vain; But a woman that feareth Jehovah, she shall be praised. [31]Give her of the fruit of her hands; And let her works praise her in the gates.

Teaching & Commentary

Realizing that we are priceless because of what Jesus has done for us. You and I are treasured in heaven and are deeply loved. Be wise, make God proud that you are in his image and be a good steward of everything he has given you.

Proverbs 30 - The Sayings of Agur

It's an odd chapter. It's one of the few in the Bible that is labeled with its author, Agur. Agur has one of the strangest introductions.

He begins by saying that he doesn't know everything. His first lesson to us is that God's Word is true and sure. Agur even goes as far as to say that there are things in life that are so astonishing and humbling.

In fact, we might even argue that the wisest thing we can ever do is to realize our limitations and the greatness of God. And what does that look like today?

Well, it means admitting we don't have it all figured out. The more we realize God's wisdom in comparison to our own, the wiser we become.

Proverbs 31 - The Sayings of King Lemuel, The Virtuous Woman

The first two verses give us the advice Lemuel was given by his mother as to leadership: to not make poor habits, and to not stay silent for those that cannot speak for themselves.

We then hear the well-known passage about the virtuous woman. She is hardworking, wise, generous, and respected. But the secret of her character isn't about her skills, but her inner strength, which comes from fearing God: "a woman who fears the LORD is to be praised."

In many ways this chapter should not be taken as merely a chapter for women. No, it is not an accident that a woman is highlighted in a book that is almost exclusively about man's relationship to God. It gives a word for every person who wants to run their race well, who longs to be effective and be the best version of themselves, and it teaches us the importance of character over appearance and accomplishment.

Bottom Line:

Finishing well isn't about perfection—it's about humility, integrity, and a heart that honors God. When you build your life on His wisdom, you leave a legacy that lasts.

Let's Talk About It

1. What stood out to you in Agur's humble perspective?

2. Why do you think the Proverbs 31 woman is praised so highly?

3. What does it look like to fear the Lord in your daily life?

4. How do you want to finish this study—and this season—in a way that honors God?

Apply It to Your Life

- **Day 1:** Reflect on areas where you need to rely on God's understanding instead of your own.

- **Day 2:** Write down qualities of character you admire in others and want to grow in yourself.

- **Day 3:** Pray for God to shape your heart and help you finish this season well.

- **Day 4:** Identify one step you can take to build a lasting legacy of faith.

Think About It & Do It

- **Humility Journal:** Each day, write something you're learning or an area where you need God's help.

- **Verse Meditation:** Spend 5 minutes repeating Proverbs 31:30.

- **Heart Check:** Ask, *Am I valuing what God values most?*

Memory Verse

"Charm is deceptive, and beauty is fleeting; but a woman who fears the LORD is to be praised."
 - Proverbs 31:30

📖 It's time to Journal!

Reflect on how this week's teaching speaks to your current season of life. Now write it down.

Let's Pray

Lord, thank You for this journey through Proverbs. Help me take these lessons to heart and live with wisdom, humility, and purpose. May my life honor You in every season.

In Jesus' name, Amen

You made it!

Look how far God has brought you. This isn't the end of your study; it's the start of walking in wisdom every day.

Encouragement

Dear Friend,

Congratulations on completing your 8-week journey through the Book of Proverbs!

What a blessing it has been to walk alongside you as you sought God's wisdom, reflected on His truths, and allowed His Word to take root in your heart. Whether this study stretched you, encouraged you, or revealed new areas for growth, one thing is certain—you are not the same person who started this journey.

Throughout this study, you have learned what it means to walk in wisdom, to guard your heart, to tame your tongue, to choose the path of righteousness, and to honor God in every area of your life. These are not just lessons for a season, they are principles for a lifetime.

As you close this chapter, I encourage you not to stop here. Keep seeking God's wisdom daily. Continue meditating on the Scriptures. Share what you've learned. Live out the truths you've embraced.

He taught me and said to me, "Let your heart hold fast my words; keep my commandments, and live." — Proverbs 4:4 (ESV)

On behalf of Bridging The Gaps Ministry Inc., we celebrate your commitment, your growth, and your perseverance. We are praying that the seeds planted over these past 8 weeks will bear lasting fruit in your life, your family, and your community.

You are walking in wisdom—and your journey is just beginning.

With joy and blessings,

Bridging The Gaps Ministry Inc.

info@bridgingthegapsinc.com

#WalkingInWisdom

Why Salvation Matters?

God created us for a relationship with Him; a life filled with purpose, peace, and hope. But every one of us has sinned, falling short of God's perfect standard. Sin separates us from God and leaves us searching for meaning in things that cannot satisfy us.

The Bible says:

"For all have sinned and fall short of the glory of God."
Romans 3:23

"For the wages of sin is death, but the gift of God is eternal life in Christ Jesus our Lord."
Romans 6:23

Jesus Christ, God's Son, came to rescue us. Jesus lived a sinless life; He died on the cross to pay the penalty for our sin and rose again so we could be forgiven and have eternal life.

Believing in Jesus isn't about religion—it's about trusting the One who gave everything to save us. When we put our faith in Jesus, we then receive forgiveness, a restored relationship with God, and the promise of eternal life.

Jesus said:

"I am the way and the truth and the life. No one comes to the Father except through me."
John 14:6

Accepting Jesus is the most crucial decision you will ever make. It changes not only your eternity but the purpose and peace you can experience right now.

A Prayer of Salvation

If you are ready to trust Jesus as your Savior, you can pray this prayer sincerely from your heart:

Dear God,

I know that I am a sinner, and I need Your forgiveness. I believe that Jesus Christ died on the cross for my sins and rose again. Today, I turn away from my old life and place my faith in Jesus alone as my Savior and Lord.

Come into my heart, forgive me, and make me a new creation. I trust You and commit to follow You. Thank You for loving me and giving me eternal life.

Amen.

What to Expect After Salvation

Choosing to follow Jesus is the beginning of a new life. The Bible describes it this way:

"Therefore, if anyone is in Christ, he is a new creation. The old has passed away; behold, the new has come."
2 Corinthians 5:17

Here's what you can expect:

- ✓ Peace and Joy: You will have the peace of knowing you're forgiven and loved by God.

- ✓ The Holy Spirit: God's Spirit will live in you, guiding, comforting, and strengthening you.

- ✓ A New Identity: You are now a child of God, adopted into His family.

- ✓ Spiritual Growth: As you spend time with God, you'll see your life begin to change.

Your Next Steps

After receiving salvation, here are some key things you can do to grow in your new relationship with God:

- ✓ **Tell Someone:** Share your decision with a pastor, mentor, or trusted Christian friend.

- ✓ **Get a Bible:** Begin reading God's Word daily. The Book of John is a wonderful place to start.

- ✓ **Pray Regularly:** Talk to God honestly and often—prayer is simply a conversation with Him.

- ✓ **Find a Church:** Connect with a Bible-believing community where you can be encouraged and learn.

- ✓ **Be Baptized:** Baptism is an outward sign of your inward faith. Talk with your church about taking this step.

- ✓ **Keep Growing:** Learn, serve, and stay connected to other believers. God has a purpose for your life!

We're Here for You

If you made the decision to trust Jesus today, we'd love to celebrate with you and help you take your next steps.

✉ **Contact Us:**
Bridging the Gaps Ministry
contact@bridgingthegapsinc.com

You are not alone on this journey!

1. What is one major truth about God you learned from Proverbs?

2. Which topic affected you the most (trust, speech, correction, etc.)?

3. Describe a situation where you applied biblical wisdom during this study.

4. What personal growth have you noticed in how you speak, decide, or relate to others?

5. Which area of wisdom do you still want to develop further?

6. List one habit or change you want to continue practicing.

7. Write a prayer of gratitude for the journey God has brought you through.

Nicole Marioneaux is a woman of faith and purpose, passionate about helping others experience God's wisdom in every area of life.

Through Bridging The Gaps Ministry Inc., she creates Christ-centered studies and devotionals designed to make Scripture practical, personal, and powerful.

Her desire is that every reader will grow closer to God, discover their identity in Christ, and walk daily in wisdom, grace, and confidence.

Bridging The Gaps Ministry Inc. exists to equip, encourage, and empower believers to live with purpose and spiritual wisdom.

Our mission is to help individuals bridge the gap between where they are and where God is calling them to be — spiritually, emotionally, and practically.

Through Bible studies, devotionals, wellness resources, and faith-based tools, we help men, women, and families grow in their walk with Christ.

"And they that shall be of thee shall build the old waste places: thou shalt raise up the foundations of many generations; and thou shalt be called, The repairer of the breach, The restorer of paths to dwell in."

— **Isaiah 58:12 (KJV)**

To learn more or access additional study resources, reach out to us @: Contact@bridgingthegapsinc.com

Scripture quotations are taken from the **Holy Bible, King James Version (KJV)**, Public Domain, and the **American Standard Version (ASV, 1901)**, Public Domain.

A complete copy of the Book of Proverbs (ASV) is provided within this publication by permission of **Paper.Bible**, a free public domain Bible resource. (Visit www.paper.bible for additional versions and study tools.)

Additional references and study insights were drawn from the following sources to support the Walking in Wisdom: An 8-Week Bible Study for Women curriculum:

1. The Holy Bible, King James Version (KJV), Public Domain.
2. The Holy Bible, American Standard Version (ASV, 1901), Public Domain.
3. The New Strong's Exhaustive Concordance of the Bible, James Strong, Thomas Nelson Publishers.
4. Vine's Expository Dictionary of Biblical Words, W.E. Vine, Thomas Nelson Publishers.
5. Matthew Henry's Commentary on the Whole Bible, Hendrickson Publishers.
6. The Moody Bible Commentary, The Moody Bible Institute.
7. NIV Study Bible, Zondervan Publishing.
8. The Bible Exposition Commentary, Warren W. Wiersbe, David C. Cook.
9. Tyndale Bible Dictionary, Tyndale House Publishers.
10. Blue Letter Bible (www.blueletterbible.org) — used for Greek/Hebrew study and cross-references.
11. Bible Gateway (www.biblegateway.com) — used for scripture comparison and topical searches.
12. Paper.Bible (www.paper.bible) — for access to the public-domain American Standard Version text.

www.ingramcontent.com/pod-product-compliance
Lightning Source LLC
LaVergne TN
LVHW041233080426
835508LV00011B/1189